CW00671659

Text compiled by Jean Watson
This edition copyright © 2003 Lion Publishing

Published by
Lion Publishing plc
Mayfield House, 256 Banbury Road,
Oxford OX2 7DH, England
www.lion-publishing.co.uk
ISBN 0 7459 4816 2

First edition 2003
10 9 8 7 6 5 4 3 2 1 0

Acknowledgments

Every effort has been made to trace and contact copyright owners
for material used in this book. We apologize for any inadvertent
omissions or errors, and would ask those concerned to contact us
so that full acknowledgment can be made in the future.

A catalogue record for this book is available
from the British Library

Typeset in 12/15 Lapidary 333
Printed and bound in Finland

Inside Stories

Tales of change and growth

Compiled by Jean Watson

A LION BOOK

Contents

Introduction

Everything in life that we really accept undergoes a change.
So suffering must become love. That is the mystery.
Katherine Mansfield

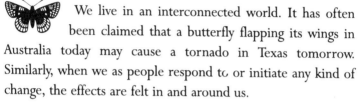 We live in an interconnected world. It has often been claimed that a butterfly flapping its wings in Australia today may cause a tornado in Texas tomorrow. Similarly, when we as people respond to or initiate any kind of change, the effects are felt in and around us.

In what follows, aspects of change and growth are illustrated through fiction, biography, poetry and reflective or analytical prose extracts: pieces that explore both our 'inside' and our 'outside' stories – the people we become, our way of life and the influence we have on ourselves, others and our world.

Jean Watson

The whole material world is preserved by gravity or attraction, or the mutual tendency of all bodies to each other. One part of the universe is hereby made beneficial to another; the beauty, harmony and order, regular progress, life and motion, and in short all the well-being of the whole frame depends on it.

Jonathan Edwards

His biographer said...

Young Ian is a member of a supposedly ideal American family, daydreaming about being famous.

Since every human soul is unique, the light that it sees and the light that it shines have never been seen or shone before.

Philip Toynbee

His father claimed Ian had talent. In fact, sometimes Ian daydreamed about pitching for the Orioles, but he knew he didn't have *that* much talent. He was a medium kind of guy, all in all.

Even so, there were moments when be believed that someday, somehow, he was going to end up famous. Famous for what, he couldn't quite say; but he'd be walking up the back steps or something and all at once he would imagine a camera zooming in on him, filming his life story. He imagined the level, cultured voice of his biographer saying, 'Ian climbed the steps. He opened the door. He entered the kitchen.'

'Had a good day, hon?' his mother asked, passing through with a laundry basket.

'Oh,' he said, 'the usual run of scholastic triumphs and athletic glories.' And he set his books on the table.

His biographer said, 'He set his books on the table.'

Anne Tyler

What's in a name?

What am I after all but a child, pleased with the sound of
    my own name? repeating it over and over;
I stand apart to hear – it never tires me.

To you your name also;
Did you think there was nothing but two or three
    pronunciations in the sound of your name?

Walt Whitman

All that I am

I am the part that I must play,
I am the journey I must go,
All that I am I must endure
And bear the burden of my years
Of good and evil, time and place,
Before the story all is told.
All that is possible must be
Before the concord can be full
Of earth's great cry of joy and woe.

Kathleen Raine

Why aren't we dancing?

You start out as a single cell derived from the coupling of a sperm and an egg; this divides into two, then four, then eight, and so on, and at a certain stage there emerges a single cell which will have as all its progeny the human brain. The mere existence of that cell should be one of the great astonishments of the earth. One cell is switched on to become the whole trillion-cell, massive apparatus for thinking and imagining and, for that matter, for being surprised. All the information needed for learning to read and write, playing the piano, arguing before senatorial committees, walking across a street through traffic, or the marvellous human act of putting out one hand and leaning against a tree, is contained in that first cell.

Statistically, the probability of any of us being here is so small that you'd think the mere fact of existing would keep us all in a contented dazzlement of surprise. We are alive against the stupendous odds of genetics. We violate probability by our nature. Add to this the biological improbability that makes each member of our own species unique. Everyone is one in three billion at the moment, which describes the odds. Each of us is a self-contained, free-standing individual, labelled by specific protein configurations at the surface of cells, identifiable by whorls of fingertip skin, maybe even by special medleys of fragrance. You'd think that we'd never stop dancing.

Breath of life

Once upon a legendary time, in the island of Cyprus, there lived a man called Pygmalion. He was a highly skilled sculptor, who lived for his work. Even so, there were times when he felt sad and lonely. One day, he had an idea. He would fashion a companion for himself – a truly beautiful woman. He prayed to the goddess Venus to help him with his work – and she did.

Pygmalion was enchanted with his statue. He named her Galatea and wanted to be with her all the time, for he had fallen in love with her. This turned his joy into anguish, for she could not love him in return. If only he could bring her to life!

'Venus, goddess of love,' he prayed, 'please take pity on me and bestow the gift of life on my beloved.'

That evening, Pygmalion was sitting near the statue, his heart ready to break, when he heard a soft voice calling his name. He spun round and there was Galatea walking towards him, smiling and holding out her arms. Pygmalion ran to embrace her.

Galatea told him, 'I woke to hear a lovely lady telling me, "Galatea, life without love is a gift of little worth." Then she kissed me and said, "With this kiss receive from me the power to love as you are loved." With that she disappeared, and here I am – brought to life by your love.'

Greek myth, retold by Jean Watson

Enquire within

A glimpse into the growing pains and dilemmas of thirteen-year-old Jessica.

'What should I do? Just tell me what to do and I'll do it.' I was too worn out to assert my independence. I just wanted her to gather me up and rock me like I was her baby again and make it all better.

'Uh-uh. Come 'ere,' she said, and pulled me over to the mirror. I looked at the puffy-eyed, runny-nosed monster staring back at me. 'No matter who you're friends with, no matter what you do, *that's* who you'll have to face every day for the rest of your life. Decide what you need to do to make *that* person proud.'

She gave me a kiss and walked out of my room.

But what if I'm *not* proud, Mom? I know I have to like myself, but what if I honestly don't? What if my real self is just not likeable? What if who I am doesn't fit in and doesn't know what to do with her hands and wears queer clothes? Then don't I have to change who I am? But if I can just change, then who is me?

Rachel Vail

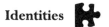

Whoever I am

Who am I? They often tell me
I would step from my cell's confinement
Calmly, cheerfully, firmly,
Like a squire from his country house.
Who am I? They often tell me
I used to speak to my warders
Freely and friendly and clearly,
As though it were mine to command.
Who am I? They also tell me
I bore the day's misfortune
Equably, smilingly, proudly,
Like one accustomed to win.
Am I then really all that which other men tell of?
Or am I only what I myself know of myself,
Restless and longing and sick, like a bird in a cage?
Who am I? This or the other?
Am I one person today and tomorrow another?
Am I both at once? A hypocrite before others,
And before myself a contemptibly woebegone weakling?
Or is something within me still like a beaten army,
Fleeing in disorder from victory already achieved?
Who am I? They mock me, these lonely questions of mine.
Whoever I am, thou knowest, O God, I am thine!

Dietrich Bonhoeffer

Betwixts and betweens

Silvia Rodgers brings together the aspects of her nature and nurture that contribute to making her the person she is.

I was born in the Berlin that Stephen Spender called 'the centre of the world', yet I was always off-centre. I was a Polish child in the German capital, a Communist child in a Fascist state, a Jewish child in a German school, an atheist child in a Jewish orthodox school, a refugee child in England, and later, when I was the wife of a British MP, Cabinet Minister, cofounder of a new party, peer of the realm, I may have looked an insider, but that was misleading...

I have been forced by political circumstance to face up to all sorts of betwixts and betweens. Being born a Jew and a woman and a foreigner, I was marginal from the start. I like the coincidence that I was born in the Weimar Republic and on the site of the Berlin Wall. A coincidence no doubt, but could it have been an omen? As if a mischievous fairy had placed me there to avenge the atheism and rationality of my secular mother who denied fairies as she denied God. Whereas God punishes the son, mischievous fairies punish the daughter, and always at birth and with a gift. Red hair was one such gift, symbols of marginality another. In Nazi Germany, this marginality was highly dangerous. But in England I have come to glory in it as a gift.

Silvia Rodgers

Open to surprise

I alone can't ask to be seen fully for who I am and my unique value. If I want you to acknowledge my gifts, I have to be curious about yours. I have a responsibility to look for and honour yours. We create enough space for our own self-expression only by inviting in everybody else's uniqueness.

Whenever we get past the categories and stereotypes, when we greet each other as interesting individuals, we are always surprised by who we are. I'm sure you've had the experience of stereotyping someone because of their appearance, and then being surprised when they didn't fit that judgment. This has happened to me so often you'd think I wouldn't keep labelling people – a labourer in ill-fitting clothes who talked with me about his love of Shakespeare, a youth with brightly dyed blue hair and body piercings who described his work teaching non-violence to young children, a factory worker who shared her poetry, a desperately poor village woman who invited me in to her immaculate, one-room home. But still I am surprised. When will I be free of these categories that prevent me from enjoying who you are?

Margaret J. Wheatley

 **Identities**

Stranger than fiction

We men are from one point of view mere trivial microbes, but from another the crown of creation: both views are true, and we must hold them together, interpenetrating, in our thought. From the point of view of the stellar universe, whose size and meaningless spaces baffle comprehension and belief, man may appear a mere nothing, and all his efforts destined to disappear like the web of a spider brushed down from the corner of a little room in the basement of a palace; but meanwhile he is engaged upon a task which by him can be imagined, the task of imposing mind and spirit upon matter and outer force. This he does by confronting the chaos of outer happenings with his intellect and generating ordered knowledge; with his aesthetic sense, and generating beauty; with his purpose, and generating control of nature; with his ethical sense and his sense of humour, and generating character; with his reverence, and generating religion.

Julian Huxley

The self *is* – one might say – what the past is doing now. It is continuity; and so it is necessarily memory – continuity seen as the shape of a unique story, my story which I now own, acknowledge, as mine. To be a self is to own such a story: to act as a self is to act out of the awareness of this resource of a particular past.

Rowan Williams

Back to the future

Dorinda tries to run away from her past. But, at the age of eighteen, she returns — to face herself, her family and her roots.

'Not conscious,' she muttered. 'Not conscious…' That was what she so often was, back in the old days. Blank, Dorinda, blank; her mantra, her escape. There was no time for that now, too much to do, too many things to think about. Nevertheless she sat on, gazing ahead, thinking of nothing in particular, everything at once, quite still, but not quite blank. The shadows of the palings cut regular sharp trenches on the yard; the intensely red brick of the station building burned into her mind. Images for her sketch book, stored away for later use.

A shrill bell rang from the station, breaking into Dorinda's thoughts. She unfolded herself from the car and strolled across the yard as the little train came chug-chugging into the station. And Dorinda waited, repeating to herself the words she knew by heart:

> … *who has arrived*
>
> *after long journeying where he*
> *began, catching this*
> *one truth by surprise*
>
> *that there is everything to look forward to.*

Dorinda Murphy, back where she began, after long and painful journeyings, caught herself grinning with delight, looking forward, now, to everything.

Bette Paul

Pain threshold

Matt, an archivist, meets and marries a woman whose tragic experiences have led to an obsession with pain and evil.

Judith was the only fully awake person I'd ever known. She watched and listened; she paid attention. History was anything but abstract for her, and she couldn't defend herself against it. The war wasn't somewhere else, at some other time. It was irrevocably present for her. The terrible things that had been done, not randomly but under unimaginably well-organized circumstances – these were realities her psyche couldn't encompass or deflect. Europe's crisis set her adrift. It became impossible for her to distinguish between the world's darkness and her own.

By the end, her body reflected everything. She'd been for too long at too high a pitch. She could no longer modulate any of her emotions. In our last encounter she would hear nothing of solace or grace. My words were like fuel on flames, and I could say nothing that wouldn't injure her further.

Martha Cooley

Give sorrow words

The sooner survivors are given an opportunity to discuss in detail what has happened to them the better. Peter Hodgkinson says: 'This generally helps them begin to put their mental house in order. They can then start to process their thoughts about it.' The problems do not become ingrained and are easier to deal with. In order to process the thoughts of the disaster properly, it is necessary for the survivors to talk about what has happened to them in depth and with full and genuine feeling.

The vast majority of disaster survivors come to terms with their experiences in time. Psychologists believe, however, that they are unlikely to get down to the general anxiety level they had before the disaster.

Dr James Thomson says: 'Many survivors ask me, "Will I be like I was?" I say to them, "The person you will be is probably a close relative to the person you might have been anyway." The key to good psychological adjustment is knowing when to kiss something goodbye, knowing when an issue is not worth thrashing about. Having thought about an event, and got rid of it, kiss it goodbye and put it behind you.'

Geraldine Sheridan and Thomas Kenning

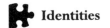

Doing love

There's only what you do.
Everything else is inside your head.

But what you do is just the expression
of who you are
and what you know.

And what you do covers a multitude of sins.
You do your tone of voice.

You do the silences between your words
as well as the words themselves.
You do the songs you sing.
You do the cup of tea you made your mum.
You do the way you spend your money
and the way you didn't spend it.
You do the love you make
and all the love you didn't make.
You do the atmosphere you change within a room.
You do the rocking of the baby in your arms.

But... what you do is the expression
of who you are
and what you know.

If what you are feels wrong or not worth much,
scrunched up in a miserable little ball,
it goes without saying that what you do will mirror that.
And what others do you will receive
much the same.

Kathy Galloway

You don't say!

I cannot help believing that the world will be a better and a
happier place when people are praised more and blamed less;
when we utter in their hearing the good we think and also gently
intimate the criticisms we hope may be of service. For the world
grows smaller every day. It will be but a family circle after
a while.

Francis E. Willard

We are different so that we can know our need of one another,
for no one is ultimately self-sufficient. A completely self-sufficient
person would be sub-human.

Desmond Tutu

Sum

I am
who and what I
treasure worship hate fear
my genes and gender
my birth and my giving birth
my relationships and how I relate
who and what I know and don't
what I do and what is done to me
what I think and what is thought about me
the words spoken and made flesh
by me to me for me
the music I have heard and made
what I remember or forget
where I am and where I have been
my pains and pleasures
strengths and weaknesses
achievements and struggles
what I live for
and what I would die for
my way of looking at life
my faith prayers dreams hopes
my choices and responses
what I create and what created me

I am
your love for me
my love for you
especially that
my dearest heavenly earthly
loves and friends
especially that

Jean Watson

Till we have faces

Love is not an option for human beings, it is a requirement. It is the most profound statement of who we are. But in this world our love will always be incomplete. Our intimacy will always be partial. For we are contending with brokenness and sin, which can hurt and destroy. We are looking through a glass darkly, but one day we shall be face to face. Yet though the glass is dark it still reflects; it still tells us whose image we bear; it shows us that we are made in love. It is only when we give ourselves up to that love that we can come to know who we are, and all we can be. In the closeness of intimacy we begin to have faces.

Elaine Storkey

Shaping up

One of the main shaping forces on our identity is our moral values. From these come our sense of meaning and purpose in life. Some things are more valuable than others. Something is worth living for; perhaps something is even worth dying for.

The second shaping factor to our sense of identity is models. Your models are those people or images of people that you would like to be like; it would be heroic to be like them.

A third factor is dominion: mastery over some bit of the world to some degree. It would include a child learning mastery over his own body in learning to crawl, walk, talk, or ride a bicycle. It would include designing an aeroplane, writing a poem, or making a relationship grow. In the modern world especially, our use of language is one of the main areas of dominion.

Lastly there is the factor of love. This is closely related to dominion, but needs to be treated separately. Love given and received is vital to our sense of self. If we do not love, we are very much less than we were made to be. If we do love, our sense of identity grows.

Dick Keyes

Growing pains

'What is REAL?' asked the Rabbit one day, when they were lying side by side near the nursery fender, before Nana came to tidy the room. 'Does it mean having things that buzz inside you and a stick-out handle?'

'Real isn't how you are made,' said the Skin Horse. 'It's a thing that happens to you. When a child loves you for a long, long time, not just to play with, but REALLY loves you, then you become Real.'

'Does it hurt?' asked the Rabbit.

'Sometimes,' said the Skin Horse, for he was always truthful. 'When you are Real you don't mind being hurt.'

'Does it happen all at once, like being wound up,' the Rabbit asked, 'or bit by bit?'

'It doesn't happen all at once,' said the Skin Horse. 'You become. It takes a long time. That's why it doesn't often happen to people who break easily, or have sharp edges, or who have to be carefully kept. Generally, by the time you are Real, most of your hair has been loved off, and your eyes drop out and you get loose in the joints and very shabby. But these things don't matter at all, because once you are Real you can't be ugly, except to people who don't understand.'

Marjorie Williams

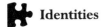

Getting real

Georgie finds the courage to tell the truth that will set her free.

I walk to the front of the room, and I start.

' "When angry, count four; when very angry, swear." Mark Twain wrote that years and years ago – he was a clever guy most of the time, but that piece of advice was dumb. I know. I did it. And it got me into big trouble...'

They are listening.

'My mother is in a psychiatric hospital.' I pause. I can hear the odd gasp.

'I was stupid enough to believe that it was something to be ashamed about, something to keep secret. But it's not. It's no more shameful than having a broken leg or German measles or a face full of acne... When we talked about mental health in class, I got really uptight. That's when I lost it – self-control.'

I take a deep breath. 'I have told a load of lies lately – I'm not having tests in hospital, my mum isn't abroad and there won't be a birthday party on Saturday... Self-control is about facing up to facts in a dignified way, and from now on that is what I shall be doing. I lashed out in class and I'm sorry. Really.'

I've finished.

I sit down.

Suddenly everyone is clapping.

Rosie Rushton

Job of work

If a man is called to be a streetsweeper, he should sweep streets even as Michelangelo painted, or Beethoven composed music, or Shakespeare wrote poetry. He should sweep streets so well that all the hosts of heaven and earth will pause to say: 'Here lived a great streetsweeper who did his job well.'

Martin Luther King Jr

Room to move

don't establish the
boundaries
first,
the squares, triangles,
boxes
of preconceived
possibility,
and then
pour
life into them, trimming
off leftover edges,
ending potential:

A.R. Ammons

Viewpoints

Bedsit

**Depends
on what
you look at,
obviously,
but even
more it
depends
on the
way that
you see.**

Bruce Cockburn

Seated
By the one-bar electric fire
In the one room
Someone else somehow calls home
 (the grease stain from a badly packed
 takeaway chow mein
 spreading on the knee of my jeans,
 rock music spilling into the unwarmed air
 from a transistor radio on the floor)
I'm drinking coffee.
Always drinking coffee.

And in how many rooms
Around the fringes of the capital
Do other girls eat mock-Chinese food,
And, coffee-drugged,
Sit up late on floor cushions,
Discussing what he said last night
 and how they lost a pound by missing lunch
  three days last week
 and how they'd look without a fringe,
And, having talked their hearts away,
Walk, haloed by the street lights,
Back to their own one-room world,

Looking to the next night's conviviality
To take away the pain
Of the never-ending
Search for something more?

Sue Elkins

Master story

A table or chair just 'is', but a human being needs to feel that he exists in terms of something, some standard or point of integration. A woman could be single, often be depressed, could earn an average income, be resentful of her father, and have an optimistic view of her country's future. However, these are temporary features of her life. Any one of them can change and none of them is large enough or solid enough to be the core of her identity. But the question remains, what *does* she relate to? How does she come to grips with the reality which is her? To adequately deal with these questions she needs to know what kind of world she is living in, and what her place in it is; she needs to know what she values, whether she has any conscious control over her life, and if there is any self worth searching for. One writer speaks of each of us having a 'master story' – some kind of picture of what the world is like and how it works. In the light of this story we interpret the meaning of our lives.

Dick Keyes

Speaking in parables

Our lives are not a random series of events; they tell a Story that has meaning. We aren't in a movie we've arrived at twenty minutes late; we are in a Sacred Romance. There really is something wonderful that draws our heart; we are being wooed. But there is also something fearful. We face an enemy with vile intentions. Is anyone in charge? Someone strong and kind who notices us? At some point we have all answered that question 'no' and gone on to live in a smaller story. But the answer is *'yes'* – there is someone strong and kind who notices us. Our Story is written by God who is more than author; he is the romantic lead in our personal dramas. He created us for himself and now he is moving heaven and earth to restore us to his side. His wooing seems wild because he seeks to free our heart from the attachments and addictions we've chosen.

And we – who are we, really? We are not pond scum, nor are we the lead in the story. We are the Beloved; our hearts are the most important thing about us and our desire is wild because it is made for a wild God. We are faced with a decision that grows with urgency each passing day: will we leave our small stories behind and venture forth to follow our Beloved into the Sacred Romance? The choice to become a pilgrim of the heart can happen any day and we can begin our journey from any place. We are here, the time is now, and the Romance is always unfolding.

Brent Curtis and John Eldredge

A mystery story

Barnaby and Maud May are having a conversation about God, catastrophes and suffering.

'In the afterlife,' Maud May told me, 'God's got a lot of explaining to do.'

'What about?' I asked. I was unpacking groceries and she was smoking a cigarette at her kitchen table.

'Oh,' she said, 'children suffering, cancer, tidal waves, tornadoes…'

'You think those need explaining? Tornadoes just happen, man. You think God sits around aiming tornadoes at people on purpose?'

'… old ladies breaking their hips and becoming a burden…'

'The most he might explain is how to *deal* with a tornado,' I said. 'How to accept it or endure it or whatever; how to do things right. That's what I'm going to ask about when I get to heaven myself: how to do things right.'

Then I said, 'Anyhow. You're not an old lady.'

'Good Gawd, Barnaby, you've gone and bought those god-damned generic tea bags again!'

I looked at the box I was holding. I said, 'Rats. I thought they were Twinings.'

'Interesting that you imagine you'll get *into* heaven,' Maud May said wryly.

Anne Tyler

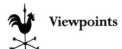

Viewpoints

Pictures in my head

At seven, when I go to bed,
I find such pictures in my head;
Castles with dragons prowling round,
Gardens where magic fruits are found;
Fair ladies prisoned in a tower,
Or lost in an enchanted bower;
While gallant horsemen ride by streams
That border all their land of dreams
I find so clearly in my head
At seven, when I go to bed.

Robert Louis Stevenson

The eye of the beholder

Why is it that, thousands of years later, Helen of Troy's story still
has the power to haunt us? Isn't it that we long to believe beauty
really could do that – there really might be someone worth
launching a thousand ships to regain and someone willing, out
of passionate love, to launch those ships? Could it be that we,
all of us, the homecoming queens and quarterbacks and the
passed-over and picked-on, really possess hidden greatness? Is
there something in us worth fighting over?

Brent Curtis and John Eldredge

Storylines

Ursula Hegi's heroine is a dwarf called Trudi living in a small German town during the Second World War. Cut off by her size from many aspects of life, she reads books and watches people avidly. Here are some of her comments about the stories in the library where she works.

'There are five basic plots in these books.' She counted them off on her fingers. 'One, true love overcomes all obstacles and becomes eternal love; two, cowboys and Indians smoke peace pipes together after they've fought over territories; three, beautiful nurses and brilliant doctors save incurable patients and then get married; four, war heroes conquer their enemies in spectacular battles; and five, villains are always punished.'

In real life, she knew, it was not that easy to tell who the villains were, and even if you could identify them, they were not total villains. No one was entirely all of one thing. Cowards could be courageous in some matters, and love was not always declared and might not be pure love, but mixed in with hate and fear and a powerful wish for revenge.

Ursula Hegi

Text message

Clementine is a chronic worrier, but longs to change. The question is how? As she works on a collection of fairy tales, she reflects on what they have to say about change.

The more she immersed herself in the fairy tales, the more she thought of how transformation was at the heart of each and every one of them. The weak became strong; the ugly, beautiful; the poor, rich; the cowards, brave; people changed. Their lives were turned round. These stories, she thought, were really just old-fashioned self-help manuals, of the you-can-do-anything-you-set-your-mind-to variety; drastic ones, maybe, giving drastic but not always practical advice: so you don't like your work as a kitchen hand, well, stay cool, stay sweet, find a fairy and go to a party. Or, more down to earth: you fancy this really beautiful girl, but she won't even look at you because, not putting too fine a point on it, you're as ugly as sin. Now, don't worry. Engineer a situation where you have to spend a lot of time together. Show her your gentle, caring, romantic side and before you know it, to her you'll appear a beautiful prince. People can change; these stories said, love conquers all; no wonder fairy tales were synonymous with unobtainable dreams.

Marika Cobbold

Heart of gold

The reason we enjoy fairy tales – more than enjoy them – the reason we *identify with them* in some deep part of us is because they rest on two great truths: the hero really has a heart of gold and the beloved really possesses hidden beauty.

The theme of veiled identity runs through all great stories. The heroines and heroes capture our heart because we see long before they ever do their hidden beauty, courage, greatness. Cinderella, Sleeping Beauty, Snow White: they're not simple wenches after all. The beast and the frog – they're actually princes. Things are rarely what they seem; we shouldn't be fooled by appearances.

Brent Curtis and John Eldredge

Seeking inspiration

I think we all want to be able to identify with the major character in a book – to live, suffer, dream and grow through vicarious experience. I need to be able to admire the protagonist despite his faults, and so be given a glimpse of my own potential. We don't want to feel *less* when we have finished a book; we want to feel that new possibilities of being have been opened to us. We don't want to close a book with a sense that life is totally unfair and that there is no light in the darkness; we want to feel that we have been given illumination.

Madeleine L'Engle

Viewpoints

A tiger to tea

At our house we have wondered if the silvery dewy spider webs in the early morning sun had been part of the decorations for a ball the fairies held the night before, especially if some toadstools had sprung up in the same area. We discussed it as if it were true, but it was like sharing a special secret. We all knew it was make-believe. There is nothing unspiritual about an active imagination, a token of the liberty of childhood.

One of my young friends, at three, told me about the tiger who lived in her back yard. I inquired about where she kept him and what she fed him, and she told me the details with great delight. Then I told her about the tiger who lived in my back yard. Her eyes danced as I described his strange behaviour. Then she came very close and whispered, 'Is yours a real one?' When I said it wasn't, she said confidentially, 'Mine isn't either.'

Was I encouraging her to lie? I think not. Both of us were in on the world of pretend – a legitimate adventure. How quickly we want to quench the fine spirit of childhood! Imagination is the stuff out of which creativity comes, and this little girl's artwork already shows a skilful amount of this rare ingredient.

Gladys Hunt

The last freedom

On his time in a Nazi concentration camp, Victor Frankl writes:

The experiences of camp life show that a man does have a choice of action. There were enough examples, often of a heroic nature, which proved that apathy could be overcome, irritability suppressed. Man can preserve a vestige of spiritual freedom, of independence of mind, even in such terrible conditions of psychic and physical stress. We who lived in concentration camps can remember the men who walked through the huts comforting others, giving away their last piece of bread. They may have been few in number, but they offer sufficient proof that everything can be taken away from a man but one thing: the last of the human freedoms – to choose one's attitude in any given circumstances, to choose one's way. The way in which a man accepts his fate and all the suffering it entails, the way in which he takes up his cross, gives him ample opportunity – even in the most difficult circumstances – to add a deeper meaning to his life.

Victor Frankl

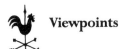

Viewpoints

A long silence

A young colleague comes into my office. He explains to me that he has all at once come to a decisive turning point in his life. He has worked enthusiastically for some years on scientific research. Now he has been obliged by circumstances to leave his research team. It is not going to be easy for him to find as interesting a post as the one he has left. Perhaps he will waste precious years waiting for it to turn up. But if he turns to a different type of work, even temporarily, he is running the risk of finding it impossible ever to go back to the sort of adventure in research that he has just been engaged in. I question him: 'What do you want to do most of all in the world?' There is a long silence. And then he replies: 'I want to do something worthwhile.'

Paul Tournier

What if?

What if we discover that our
present way of life is
irreconcilable with our vocation
to become fully human?

Paulo Freire

Wish list

May I be no man's enemy, and may I be the friend of that which is eternal and abides.

May I never quarrel with those nearest me; and if I do, may I never devise evil against any man; if any devise evil against me, may I escape uninjured and without the need of hurting him.

May I love, seek and attain only that which is good.

May I wish for all men's happiness and envy none.

May I never rejoice in the ill-fortune of one who has wronged me.

When I have done or said what is wrong, may I never wait for the rebuke of others, but always rebuke myself until I make amends.

May I win no victory that harms either me or my opponent.

May I reconcile friends who are wroth with one another.

May I, to the extent of my power, give all needful help to my friends and to all who are in want.

May I never fail a friend in danger.

When visiting those in grief, may I be able by gentle and healing words to soften their pain.

May I respect myself.

May I accustom myself to be gentle, and never be angry with people because of circumstances.

May I never discuss who is wicked and what wicked things he has done, but know good men and follow in their footsteps.

Eusebius

Third peacock on the left

We can long for a world free from risks, danger, pain and suffering. But what kind of a world would it be? Peter Kreeft explores the implications.

The princess is under the curse. She is asleep and cannot be awakened except by an apple from the tree in the middle of the garden at the Western End of the World. The king gets out his maps, briefs his generals and sends a couple of well-supplied divisions to the garden to fetch the apple. The apple is brought to the palace and applied to the princess. She wakes up, eats breakfast, lunch and dinner forever after and dies in bed at the age of eighty-two.

He goes on to say that everyone knows that that is not the way the story goes. The garden is only to be found on one map, and this has been drawn with magical ink and will be visible only to the person who can whistle in double stops and imitate a pair of Baltimore orioles.

Needless to say, the king's musicians fail to do this. At the point of despair, the king hears somebody walking down the road whistling double stops like a pair of Baltimore orioles. It is, of course, the miller's third son, local school dropout and radical revolutionary.

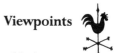

The miller's son reads the map and the warning in block capitals at the bottom: DO NOT, UNDER ANY CIRCUMSTANCES, ENGAGE IN CONVERSATION WITH THE THIRD PEACOCK ON THE LEFT.

Kreeft continues:

Any child worth his Coca-Cola can write the rest of the story for you. The boy goes into the garden and gets as far as the third peacock on the left, who asks him whether he wouldn't like a can of the local Coca-Cola. Before he knows it, he has had three and falls fast asleep. When he wakes up, he is in a pitch-black cave; a light flickers, a voice calls – and from there on all hell breaks loose. The boy follows an invisible guide wearing a cocked hat and descends into the bowels of the earth; he rows down rivers of fire in an aluminium dinghy, is imprisoned by the Crown Prince of the Salamanders, finally rescued by a confused eagle who deposits him at the *Eastern* End of the World, works his way back to the Western End in the dead of winter, gets the apple, brings it home, touches it to the princess's lips, arouses her, reveals himself as the long-lost son of the Eagle King and marries the princess. Then, and only then, do they live happily ever after.

Peter Kreeft

Living dangerously

To laugh is to risk looking a fool.
To weep is to risk appearing sentimental.
To reach out to another is to risk involvement.
To show feelings is to risk revealing your true self.
To place your ideas and dreams before a crowd
is to risk their loss.

To love is to risk rejection.
To live is to risk dying.
To hope is to risk despair.
To try is to risk failure.

But risks must be taken,
because one of the greatest dangers in life is to risk nothing.

Those who risk nothing, do nothing, achieve nothing
and become nothing.

They may avoid suffering and sorrow,
but they cannot learn, feel, change, grow, love or even live.
Chained by their uncertainties, they are slaves;
they have forfeited their freedom.

Only those who risk all that they cannot keep
to gain what they can never lose are truly free.

Simon Reynolds

Reading the small print

Share everything.
Play fair.
Don't hit people.
Put things back where you found them.
Clean up your own mess.
Don't take things that aren't yours.
Say you're sorry when you hurt somebody.
Wash your hands before you eat.
Flush.
Warm cookies and cold milk are good for you.
Live a balanced life – learn some and think some and draw
and paint and sing and dance and play and work every day some.
Take a nap every afternoon.
When you go out into the world, watch out for traffic,
hold hands, and stick together.
Be aware of wonder. Remember the little seed in the
Styrofoam cup: the roots go down and the plant goes up and
nobody really knows how or why, but we are all like that.
Goldfish and hamsters and white mice and even the little seed
in the Styrofoam cup – they all die. So do we.
And then remember the Dick-and-Jane books and the first
word you learned – the biggest word of all – LOOK.

Robert Fulghum

Viewpoints

Enjoying the view

A wise old man, who had lived buoyantly through four score years, was asked, 'Which is the happiest season of life?' He replied thoughtfully, 'When spring comes, and in the soft air the buds are breaking on the trees, and they are covered with blossoms, I think, how beautiful is spring! And when the summer comes, and covers the trees and bushes with heavy foliage, and singing birds mingle with the branches, I think, how beautiful is summer! When autumn loads them with golden fruit, and their leaves bear the gorgeous tint of frost, I think, how beautiful is autumn! And when it is sore winter, and there is neither foliage nor fruit, then when I look up through the leafless branches and see, as I can see in no other season, the shining stars of heaven, I think, how beautiful is the winter of life!'

Anon

The moon marks off the seasons, and the sun knows when to go down. You bring darkness, it becomes night, and all the beasts of the forest prowl. The lions roar for their prey and seek their food from God. The sun rises, and they steal away; they return and lie down in their dens. Then man goes out to his work, to his labour until evening.

The Bible (Psalm 104:19–23)

All in good time

There is a time for everything,
and a season for every activity under heaven:

a time to be born and a time to die,
a time to plant and a time to uproot,
a time to kill and a time to heal,
a time to tear down and a time to build,
a time to weep and a time to laugh,
a time to mourn and a time to dance,
a time to scatter stones and a time to gather them,
a time to embrace and a time to refrain,
a time to search and a time to give up,
a time to keep and a time to throw away,
a time to tear and a time to mend,
a time to be silent and a time to speak,
a time to love and a time to hate,
a time for war and a time for peace.

The Bible (Ecclesiastes 3:1–8)

Comparing notes

'Who is God, by the way?' asks our son.

I have bought his new uniform and sewn in his name tapes. I have packed up his lunch box and encouraged him to form his letters in the way they like at his new school. But in this important respect, I have not prepared him at all.

'Who do you think God is?' I ask my son.

'He made the world, put babies in people's tummies, that sort of thing...' he says.

'Yes, that's what some people believe.'

'Do you believe it?' he asks.

'Er.' I try never to lie to him. 'No I don't, really.'

'I do,' he chimes up.

In my head I hear my father's voice dismissing anyone stupid enough to believe in something without proof, and I look at my son, aged five, as innocent as an angel, full of certainty. And I say: 'Good for you.'

We run into difficulties with the Old Testament.

'You know Adam and Eve?' he asks one day.

'Yes...'

'What I don't understand is why it's bad to eat an apple. Apples are good for you,' he says.

I am tempted for a moment to lend God's weight to the reasons why you shouldn't do what you're told not to, but resist.

'Actually,' I say, 'I've never understood that either.'

'You'll go up to heaven soon, won't you?' my son pronounces one bedtime.

'I hope not.'

'But you will go up to heaven before me?'

'Yes.'

'But then I'll come up and we'll be together again.' He smiles and closes his eyes.

I think of my father, who proclaimed that heaven was a concept to make people put up with things in life that they shouldn't. And I think how much less terrified I would have been as a child if I had been allowed to think there was somewhere to go after death. I used to think that parents should know things, but increasingly I don't know. I used to think that faith was about having certainty; now I think perhaps I got it all the wrong way round. My little boy and I are finding out about faith together, and we are taking it step by step.

Imogen Parker

Sunrise of wonder

At the back of our brains, so to speak, there is a forgotten blaze or burst of astonishment at our own existence. The object of the artistic and spiritual life is to dig for this sunrise of wonder.

G.K. Chesterton

A chance to grow up

Maya Angelou describes what happened and how she felt when her son left home to start leading his own life.

Egos appear by setting themselves apart from other egos. Persons appear by entering into relation to other persons.

Martin Buber

Guy was moving into Mensa Sarba Hall. I had seen his room in the dormitory and it looked too small and too dark, but he loved it. For the first time in his life, he was going to live alone, away from my persistent commands. Responsible to himself and for himself.

He dragged the old trunk towards the door, but I stopped him.

'Don't lift heavy things like that. You could hurt yourself. I want you to be careful. Remember your neck.'

He put the trunk down and turned. 'Mom, I know I'm your only child and you love me.' His face was quiet and his voice calm. 'But there's something for you to remember. It is my neck and my life. I will live it whole or not at all.'

He pulled me to him and wrapped his arms around me. 'I love you, Mom. Maybe now you'll have a chance to grow up.'

Maya Angelou

Careful of me

Treading cautiously,
in case I step upon a toe or two.
Afraid to offend
   anyone who happens to be there.

Holding hands tenderly,
in case I fail to touch a heart or two.
Eager to attend
   anyone who happens to be there.

Always looking out for people.
Afraid to miss them; in case they miss me.

John Dutton

Friendly space

Hospitality means primarily the creation of a free space where
the stranger can enter and become a friend instead of an enemy.
Hospitality is not to change people, but to offer them space where
change can take place. The paradox of hospitality is that it wants to
create emptiness, not a fearful emptiness, but a friendly emptiness
where strangers can enter and discover themselves as created free;
free to sing their own songs, speak their own languages, dance their
own dances; free also to leave and follow their own vocations.

Henri Nouwen

Mixed bunch

Will opts for a quiet life, free from emotional entanglements.
But a needy, persistent boy, trailing an assortment of other people,
keeps intruding, and Will realizes that he has become involved.

Will looked at this strange little group, his gang for the day, and
tried to make some sense of it. All these ripples and connections!
He couldn't get his head round them. He was not a man given
to mystical moments, even under the influence of narcotics, but
he was very worried that he was having one now. It was making
him feel very peculiar. Some of these people he hadn't known
until today; some of them he had only known for a little while,
and even then he couldn't say that he knew them well. But here
they were anyway, one of them clutching a cardboard cut-out,
one of them in a plaster cast, one of them crying, all of them
bound to each other in ways that it would be almost impossible
to explain to anyone who had just wandered in. Will couldn't
recall ever having been caught up in this sort of messy, sprawling,
chaotic web before; it was almost as if he had been given a glimpse
of what it was like to be human. It wasn't too bad, really; he
wouldn't even mind being human on a full-time basis.

Nick Hornby

The loner

I am the loner,
The one who lives within my mind,
The soul that finds comfort hiding in ripples of thought,
The heart that aches, but knows that solace is exiled
    among imagination,
The spirit wandering free in a husk denied that freedom,
The deep eye of knowledge imprisoned by a dumb tongue,
I am always the chrysalis, never the butterfly,
For I am the loner.

Claire Pegg

Close to you

If I were to put forward the thesis that in our contemporary culture there is a deep and widespread longing for close relationships, there would be no shortage of evidence. The thousands of friendship clubs, matrimonial agencies and meeting centres all point to the fundamental desire for human warmth. There is a need which lies deep in the human psyche for the security of being loved just as we are. Yet that need is not always fulfilled. Crisis clinics, alcoholism centres, counselling agencies and divorce courts all indicate how difficult it can be for people to draw close and stay close to others.

Elaine Storkey

Heart to heart

To love at all is to be vulnerable. Love anything, and your heart will certainly be wrung and possibly be broken. If you want to make sure of keeping it intact, you must give your heart to no one, not even to an animal. Wrap it carefully round with hobbies and little luxuries; avoid all entanglements; lock it up safe in the casket or coffin of your selfishness. But in that casket – safe, dark, motionless, airless – it will change. It will not be broken; it will become unbreakable, impenetrable, irredeemable. The only place outside heaven where you can be perfectly safe from all the dangers and perturbations of love is hell.

C.S. Lewis

Listen to the language of your wounds.
Do not pine away in the pain of them,
but seek to live from the depths of them.
Make the extent of your desolation
the extent of your realm.

Jim Cotter, after Charles Williams

Declaration of intent

In his own inimitable way, Rob finally gets round to proposing to Laura.

'See, I've always been afraid of marriage because of, you know, ball and chain, I want my freedom, all that. But when I was thinking about that stupid girl I suddenly saw it was the opposite: that if you got married to someone you know you love, and you sort yourself out, it frees you up for other things. I know you don't know how you feel about me, but I do know how I feel about you. I know I want to stay with you and I keep pretending otherwise, to myself and you, and we just limp on and on. It's like we sign a new contract every few weeks or so, and I don't want that any more. And I know that if we got married I'd take it seriously, and I wouldn't want to mess about.'

'And you can make a decision about it just like that, can you? In cold blood, bang bang, if I do that, then this will happen? I'm not sure that it works like that.'

'But it *does*, you see. Just because it's a relationship, and it's based on soppy stuff, it doesn't mean you can't make intellectual decisions about it. Sometimes you just have to, otherwise you'll never get anywhere. That's where I've been going wrong. I've been letting the weather and my stomach muscles and a great chord change in a Pretenders single make up my mind for me, and I want to do it for myself.'

Nick Hornby

A beautiful truth

*In her autobiography, Helen Keller talks about how, as a
deaf and blind child, she learned the meaning of the word love.*

'What is love?' I asked.

She drew me closer to her and said, 'It is here,' pointing to
my heart. Her words puzzled me very much, because I did not
then understand anything unless I touched it.

I smelt the violets in her hand and asked, half in words,
half in signs, a question which meant, 'Is love the sweetness
of flowers?'

'No,' said my teacher.

Again I thought. The warm sun was shining on us.

'Is this not love?' I asked, pointing in the direction from
which the heat came.

A day or two afterwards, the sun had been under a cloud all
day, and there had been brief showers; but suddenly the sun
broke forth in all its southern splendour.

Again I asked my teacher, 'Is this not love?'

'Love is something like the clouds that were in the sky before
the sun came out,' she replied. Then in simpler words than
these, which at that time I could not have understood, she
explained: 'You cannot touch the clouds, you know; but you feel
the rain and know how glad the flowers and the thirsty earth are
to have it after a hot day. You cannot touch love either; but you

feel the sweetness that it pours into everything. Without love you would not be happy or want to play.'

The beautiful truth burst upon my mind – I felt that there were invisible lines stretched between my spirit and the spirit of others.

Helen Keller

Let me count the ways

How do I love thee? Let me count the ways.
I love thee to the depth and breadth and height
My soul can reach, when feeling out of sight
For the ends of being and ideal grace.
I love thee to the level of every day's
Most quiet need, by sun and candlelight.
I love thee freely, as men strive for right;
I love thee purely, as they turn from praise.
I love thee with the passion put to use
In my old griefs, and with my childhood's faith.
I love thee with a love I seemed to lose
With my lost saints – I love thee with the breath,
Smiles, tears, of all my life! – and, if God choose,
I shall but love thee better after death.

Elizabeth Barrett Browning

Green fingers

A relationship is like a garden. If it is to thrive it must be watered regularly. Special care must be given, taking into account the seasons as well as any unpredictable weather. New seeds must be sown and weeds must be pulled.

Falling in love is like springtime. It is a magical time when everything seems perfect and works effortlessly.

Throughout the summer of our love we realize our partner is not as perfect as we thought, and we have to work on our relationship. Frustration and disappointment arise; weeds need to be uprooted and plants need extra watering under the hot sun. It is no longer easy to give love and get the love we need. We need to nurture our partner's needs as well as ask for and get the love we need.

As a result of tending the garden during the summer, we get to harvest the results of our hard work. Autumn has come. It is a golden time – rich and fulfilling. We experience a more mature love that accepts and understands our partner's imperfections as well as our own.

The winter of love is a time of rest, reflection and renewal. It is a time of solitary growth when we need to look more to ourselves than to our partners for love and fulfilment. After loving and healing ourselves through the dark winter of love, then spring inevitably returns.

Leaps and bounds

Ellie broke into a run. At that moment it seemed to her, were she to leap up, she would rise from the moorings of earth and sail between the stars.

On an impulse, she jumped and called, 'Hey!' As she landed, the pavement smacked sharply through her thin soles; her cry came out like a mouse-squeak. She burst out laughing. It was true. She was in love.

Her experience of love gives her confidence to resist Quintin's cynicism.

'But, my dear child, surely you are not going to deprive yourself of all sorts of fun! These days, marriage is no more than the permanent set against which we play our romances. It's not a binding contract.'

She said quietly, 'I think it is a binding contract.'

'Oh, oh! What a little prude! You used not to be like this. Do you imagine your husband will remain faithful to you?'

'Yes. Why not?'

Quintin laughed at her. 'My dear child, husbands don't remain faithful.'

'Perhaps some husbands do.'

'You'll learn better. And don't forget, life is short: you will grow old.'

She thought of Simon and smiled: 'I'm prepared for that.'

Olivia Manning

Just as I am

Alfie has just told his friend's daughter that his grandmother has died.

Plum stares straight ahead, saying nothing. I grope for all the usual consolations.

'She was in a lot of pain towards the end. So we can be glad she doesn't have to suffer any more. She's at peace now.'

Plum says nothing.

'And it was a long life, Plum. One day we will learn to be grateful for her life. Not sad about her death.'

'She was the one person…'

'Plum? Are you –'

'The one person who I could be myself with. I know my mum wants me to be prettier. Lose weight. Do something about my hair. All that. And my dad wants me to be stronger. Tougher. Harder. Not get pushed around. Stand up for myself. All that.' She shakes her head. 'And the kids at school all want me to just crawl away and die. Just crawl away and die, Plumpster. But she was the one person who just accepted me. Who didn't care.' She laughs. 'Who actually seemed to quite like me.'

'Your mother loves you. Come on, Plum. You know she does.'

'But loving someone's not the same as *liking* them, is it? It's not the same as just accepting them for what they are. Love's all right, I guess. I don't know too much about all that. I'll settle for just being liked.'

Tony Parsons

Beneath the mask

The test of whether I am looking at myself or another person *with* my eyes or *through* them, with eyes that scan the surface or eyes that give attention, is whether I am prepared to to take time to search for the self beneath the mask. 'Mask' is not the word: it suggests something we don or remove with ease, like a fancy dress, and we are far more complex than that. Of course we wear our protective disguises, but the self of which we are conscious is but the tip of the iceberg, the rest lying buried deep in our unconscious, though like the iceberg capable of inflicting powerful damage.

This is not about some kind of potentially embarrassing mutual analysis: it is about honesty, the honest acceptance of ourselves and each other as we are, rather than as we should like to appear or as we should like others to be. To believe that you or anyone else is not complicated, often neglectful and selfish, sometimes envious, unloving, angry and full of self-pity, is to reveal a serious form of blindness. But it is equally blinkered not to know that you and everyone else have the capacity to be creative, thoughtful, courageous and self-sacrificing, funny, loving and compassionate. The recognition that is allied to love lies in accepting myself as I am, and you as you are.

Michael Mayne

With respect

None of us can truly assert that he really knows someone else, even if he has lived with him for years. Of that which constitutes our inner life we can impart even to those most intimate with us only fragments; the whole of it we cannot give, nor would they be able to comprehend it. We wander through life together in a semi-darkness in which none of us can distinguish exactly the features of his neighbour; only from time to time, through some experience that we have of our companion, or through some remark that he passes, he stands for a moment close to us, as though illuminated by a flash of lightning. Then we see him as he really is.

To know one another cannot mean to know everything about each other: it means to feel mutual affection and confidence, and to believe in one another. There is a modesty of soul which we must recognize, just as we do that of the body. The soul, too, has its clothing of which we must not deprive it, and no one has a right to say to another: 'Because we belong to each other as we do, I have a right to know all your thoughts.' In this matter giving is the only valuable process; it is only giving that stimulates. Impart as much as you can of your spiritual being to those who are on the road with you, and accept as something precious what comes back to you from them. Only those who respect the personality of others can be of real use to them.

Albert Schweitzer

Misunderstanding

Barnaby is having a phone conversation with his mother.

This was so untypical of her – I mean, the resigned and listless tone she used – that I caught myself feeling sorry for her. I remembered what she had said at Thanksgiving: how I was more her son than Dad's, more related to her. It seemed that now I was taking that in for the very first time. Poor Mom! It hadn't been much fun loving someone as thorny as me, I bet.

So when she told me she'd better hang up because she had a hair appointment, I said, 'Mom. You know what I think? I really think your hair would look great if you stopped dyeing it.'

It was meant to be a kindness, but it backfired. '*You* may not like it, but all my friends say it looks lovely!' she snapped. And then she told me goodbye and slammed the receiver down.

Well, no surprise there. Just because we were related didn't mean we were any good at understanding each other.

Anne Tyler

People you won't let go of

Taylor and her mother Alice have had a poor experience of men.
But as a result of adopting a Cherokee child named Turtle, and
of being loved by Jax, Taylor decides to make a commitment.

'Well, Taylor, that's wonderful!' Alice cries, sounding ready
enough to be wrong about men this once. She sings, 'Dum, dum
da dum,' to the tune of 'Here Comes the Bride,' and ties knots
in the stems of her flowers, pulling each one through the next to
make a crown. When it's finished she holds it out in her two
hands like the cat's cradle, then places it on Taylor's dark hair.
'There you go, all set.'

'Mama, you're embarrassing me,' Taylor says, but she leaves
the flowers where they are.

'What changed your mind about Jax?'

Taylor uses her long bouquet like a horse's tail, to swish away
gnats.

'When the social worker asked Turtle about her family today,
you know what she said? She said she didn't have one.'

'That's not right! She was confused.'

'Yeah. She's confused, because I'm confused. I *think* of Jax
and Lou Ann and Dwayne Ray, and of course you, and Mattie,
my boss at the tyre store, all those people as my family. But when
you never put a name on things, you're just accepting that it's
OK for people to leave when they feel like it.'

'They leave anyway,' Alice says. 'My husbands went like houses on fire.'

'But you don't have to *accept* it,' Taylor insists. 'That's what your family is, the people you won't let go of for anything.'

Barbara Kingsolver

The difference to me

She dwelt among the untrodden ways
Beside the springs of Dove,
A maid whom there were none to praise
And very few to love:

A violet by a mossy stone
Half hidden from the eye!
Fair as a star, when only one
Is shining in the sky.

She lived unknown, and few could know
When Lucy ceased to be;
But she is in her grave, and oh,
The difference to me!

William Wordsworth

♥ Relationships

A delicate web

How extraordinary is the situation of us mortals. Each of us is here for a brief sojourn; for what purpose he knows not, though he sometimes thinks he senses it. But without going deeper than our daily life, it is plain that we exist for our fellow men – in the first place for those upon whose smiles and welfare our happiness depends, and next for all those unknown to us personally but to whose destinies we are bound by the tie of sympathy. A hundred times a day I remind myself that my inner and outer life depend on the labours of other men, living and dead, and that I must exert myself in order to give in the same measure as I have received and am still receiving.

Albert Einstein

We ask a leaf, 'Are you complete in yourself?' And the leaf answers, 'No, my life is in the branches.' We ask the branch and the branch answers, 'No, my life is in the trunk.' We ask the trunk and it answers, 'No, my life is in the roots and the branches and the leaves.' So it is with our lives. Nothing is completely and merely individual.

Harry Emerson Fosdick

A single presence

There is conflict and anger between the members of this Irish family, but each time the three sisters meet, they come together as one.

Maggie flew over from London on the morning of the Day. Mona and Sheila met her at Dublin Airport and the three sisters drove to Great Meadow in Mona's car. They did not hurry. With the years they had drawn closer. Apart, they could be breathtakingly sharp on the others' shortcomings, but together their individual selves gathered into something very close to a single presence.

On the tides of Dublin or London they were hardly more than specks of froth, but together they were the aristocratic Morans of Great Meadow, a completed world, Moran's daughters. Each scrap of news any one of them had about themselves or their immediate family – child, husband, dog, cat, Bendix dishwasher, a new dress or pair of shoes, the price of every article they bought – was as fascinating to each other as if it were their very own; and any little thing out of Great Meadow was pure binding. Together they were the opposite of women who will nod and nod as they pretend to listen to one another, waiting for the first pause of breath to muscle in with the growing pains and glories of their own house, the impatience showing on their faces as they wait.

John McGahern

Open to one another

All mankind is of one author, and is one volume; when one man dies, one chapter is not torn out of the book, but translated into a better language; and every chapter must be so translated; God employs several translators; some pieces are translated by age, some by sickness, some by war, some by justice; but God's hand is in every translation; and his hand shall bind up all our scattered leaves again for that library where every book shall lie open to one another.

No man is an island, entire of itself; every man is a piece of the continent, a part of the main. If a clod be washed away by the sea, Europe is the less, as well as if a promontory were, as well as if a manor of thy friend's or of thine own were: any man's death diminishes me, because I am involved in mankind; and therefore never send to know for whom the bell tolls; it tolls for thee.

John Donne

Love is patient, love is kind. It does not envy, it does not boast, it is not proud. It is not rude, it is not self-seeking, it is not easily angered, it keeps no record of wrongs. Love does not delight in evil but rejoices with the truth. It always protects, always trusts, always hopes, always perseveres. Love never fails.

The Bible (I Corinthians 13:4–8)

A part to play

Now the body is not made up of one part but of many. If the foot should say, 'Because I am not a hand, I do not belong to the body,' it would not for that reason cease to be part of the body. And if the ear should say, 'Because I am not an eye, I do not belong to the body,' it would not for that reason cease to be part of the body. If the whole body were an eye, where would the sense of hearing be? If the whole body were an ear, where would the sense of smell be? But in fact God has arranged the parts in the body, every one of them, just as he wanted them to be. If they were all one part, where would the body be? As it is, there are many parts, but one body.

The Bible (1 Corinthians 12:14–20)

Like warp and woof all destinies
Are woven fast,
Linked in sympathy like the keys of an organ vast;
Pluck one thread, and the web ye mar;
Break but one
Of a thousand keys, and the paining jar
Through all will run.

John Greenleaf Whittier

Journeyings

Leaving the nest

Laurie Lee describes how he felt when, as a young man in 1934, he left his Cotswolds home and headed for London.

That first day alone steadily declined in excitement and vigour. As I tramped through the dust towards the Wiltshire Downs, a growing reluctance weighed me down. White elderblossom and dog roses hung in the hedges, blank as unwritten paper, and the hot empty road reflected Sunday's waste and indifference. High sulky summer sucked me towards it, and I offered no resistance at all. Through the solitary morning and afternoon I found myself longing for some opposition or rescue, for the sound of hurrying footsteps coming after me and family voices calling me back.

None came. I was free. I was affronted by freedom. The day's silence said, Go where you will. It's all yours. You asked for it. It's up to you now. You're on your own, and nobody's going to stop you. As I walked, I was taunted by echoes of home, by the tinkling sounds of the kitchen, shafts of sun from the windows falling across the familiar furniture, across the bedroom and the bed I had left.

When I judged it to be tea time I sat on an old stone wall and opened my tin of treacle biscuits. As I ate them I could hear mother banging the kettle on the hob and my brothers rattling their teacups. The biscuits tasted sweetly of the honeyed squalor of home – still only a dozen miles away.

Laurie Lee

Refugee

Called by a name I cannot own,
Pinned in a long car, my world
A railway, my head numbered;
I am held by angled rails.
Mother railway, why
Are there guards on your doors?
And always this examination
Of the pockets of my heart –
What can I say
Of my home or destination?

Patrick Hobbs

Immigrant

November '63: eight months in London.
I pause on the low bridge to watch the pelicans:
they float swanlike, arching their white necks
over only slightly ruffled bundles of wings,
burying awkward beaks in the lake's water.

I clench cold fists in my Marks and Spencer's jacket
and secretly test my accent once again:
St James's Park; St James's Park; St James's Park.

Fleur Adcock

 **Journeyings**

From winter to spring

A young boy, escaping from a Nazi concentration camp, prays to the God of green pastures and still waters for the only two things he really wants: 'freedom and a country where he could live in safety'.

He was not yet free! He turned and ran. The moon was shining now. If he could reach the turn of the road where it swept round a spur of rock, he might be able to dig himself into the snow before the farmer arrived on the scene.

David never knew how he managed to do it. Everything went black in front of his eyes as he lay in the snow.

Then a warm wet feeling on his face woke him up.

It was not the farmer after all! It was the dog who wanted to go with him!

It trotted along by his side, sometimes running on ahead but always returning to keep him company, and every time he spoke to it, it would wag its tail.

David breathed deeply, hardly noticing the cold bite in the air. He was David. He was free and strong. He was on the move again, yet this time he knew where he was making for. There might be many difficulties ahead before he reached his goal, but difficulties could be overcome. He still had one more promise of help left over from God, and he had the dog who was going with him of its own free will. The long winter had passed, and he was going down to meet the spring.

Ann Holm

Encounter at St Martin's

I tell a wanderer's tale, the same
I began long ago, a boy in a barn,
I am always lost in it. The place
is always strange to me. In my pocket

the wrong money or none, the wrong paper,
maps of another town, the phrase book
for yesterday's language, just a ticket
to the next station, and my instructions.

In the lobby of the Banco Bilbao
a dark woman will slip me a key, a package,
the name of a hotel, a numbered account,
the first letters of an unknown alphabet.

Ken Smith

I've seen sae mony changefu' years,
On earth I am a stranger grown;
I wander in the ways of men,
Alike unknowing and unknown.

Robert Burns

Going places

All is roads, even the way we think. It is not possible to minimize roads. They are a root fact, the keyhole, the key, the way we get into and go out of our lives. The very form and pressure of the time. It is a road civilization we live in.

To learn to draw is a road. Love is a road. Traits become roads. Even character seems to be only a road where the grades, overpasses, easements, direction, are especially well engineered for a maximum of traffic with a minimum of accidents.

What are they, these ubiquitous, overwhelming roads, going forever up and down? Every road is a wish gone out to work, carried to its market. Every road is an accumulation of persistence. It is a conjecture persisted in. Repeated use makes a road.

There is security in roads and habits, and there is freedom in roads and habits. They form regular lanes so that we can go on them without scouting all the way. But many a good thing may be found by going off a road. Advance is likely to depart from the road. All origins of new species and all sports and mutations and evolutions have had to go off a road.

Madge Jenison

The pilgrim song

Who would true valour see,
Let him come hither;
One here will constant be,
Come wind, come weather.
There's no discouragement
Shall make him once relent
His first avowed intent
To be a pilgrim.

Whoso beset him round
With dismal stories,
Do but themselves confound;
His strength the more is.
No lion can him fright,
He'll with a giant fight,
But he will have a right
To be a pilgrim.

Hobgoblin, nor foul fiend,
Can daunt his spirit:
He knows he at the end
Shall life inherit.
Then fancies fly away,
He'll fear not what men say,
He'll labour night and day
To be a pilgrim.

John Bunyan

71

 **Journeyings**

A place to rest

In John Bunyan's allegory, Christian and Hopeful encounter many difficulties and dangers as they journey to the Celestial City, but here they enjoy a welcome time of rest and refreshment.

I saw then that they went on their way to a pleasant river. Now their way lay just upon the bank of the river: here therefore Christian and his companion walked with great delight; they drank also of the water of the river which was pleasant and enlivening to their weary spirits; besides, on the banks of this river, on either side, were green trees that bore all manner of fruit; and the leaves of the trees were good for medicine; with the fruit of these trees they were also much delighted, and the leaves they ate to prevent surfeits, and other diseases that are incident to those that heat their blood by travels. On either side of the river was also a meadow, curiously beautified with lilies; and it was green all the year long. In this meadow they lay down and slept, for here they might lie down safely. When they awoke, they gathered again of the fruit of the trees, and drank again of the water of the river, and then lay down again to sleep. Thus they did several days and nights. So when they were disposed to go on (for they were not as yet at their journey's end), they ate and drank and departed.

John Bunyan

Time out

Most of us are not very good at resting. If we even pause in life, we tend to get anxious. If we slow down long enough actually to rest, emotional pain may start floating to the surface. To avoid this, we drive ourselves mercilessly. We keep the pace of life set at 'frenzy' and hope that we have the energy to continue living this way for a long time.

We also avoid rest because we derive such a disproportionate sense of value in life from the things we *do*. We do and do and do in order to feel all right about ourselves. If we pause long enough to *be*, we get agitated. If we slow down long enough actually to rest, we can become profoundly disorientated as we experience threats to our identity as a doer.

But we need rest. Rest restores us. It restores our bodies from the fatigue of constant activity and surges of adrenaline. It restores our minds from the never-ending clutter of lists of things to do. It restores our souls from the grandiose delusion that we are both indispensable and capable of performing beyond normal human limits.

Dale and Juanita Ryan

Heritage of beauty

When the days come that I must live alone in my own thoughts, and when my eyes are dimmed and cannot see the shadows on the hills cast by the clouds, and when I cannot hear the far-off sounds of hurrying streams and sheep, then will I turn my mind to those great days we spent upon the fells, and I will count them over one by one, and treasure them as jewels no one can take from me.

Days when I climbed among the lowering clouds and saw the mist come swirling up like steam; its flying streamers passing me so near I felt their ghostly fingers on my face. I will remember seeing through the clouds, drawn sudden back as curtains at the play, a distant lake, a valley brightly green, a glittering torrent down a mountain side, just glimpsed before 'twas blotted out again.

Days when the sun was hot on rock and heath, and I would lie far-up upon some ledge, hearing below those solemn murmurings, the sad, incessant voices of the Dales, and smell the moss and bracken 'neath my head. And I will dream of little mountain flowers, the butterwort with slender purple blooms, the sundew sticky with its catch of flies, the spongy mosses green and rusty red, and the cotton grasses wearing silken plumes beside some lonely tarn high in the hills.

I will remember rain, and bitter winds, the feel of clothes drenched by a stinging shower, teas at a wayside inn with some good friends, hot baths and fires, and warmth for tired limbs, and all the loveliness of home and rest.

And whilst I think of all those joyous days, of all the heights I've gained and hours I've loved, I will not envy those who take their turn in tramping manfully, in storm or fine, the hills I know, for they are a part of me; a heritage of beauty nought can spoil.

Anon

Songs in winter

There is much romance for me in the meadowlark. Its song *means* summer, hay meadows, long lazy days, fly-fishing. More than anything else, it has become for me a symbol of hope. The meadowlark returns to Colorado in the early spring, and that typically means it arrives about the same time as our major snowstorms hit. What courage; I'm sure if it were me, I'd wait until June when the weather warms up. But they come in spite of the snow, and take their place on fence posts and the tops of small trees, and begin singing. Hearing a midsummer song almost seems out of place when the flurries are whipping about your face. But that is exactly when we need it.

John Eldredge

 **Journeyings**

Going solo

There is a pleasure in the pathless woods,
There is a rapture on the lonely shore,
There is society where none intrudes,
By the deep sea, and music in its roar:
I love not man the less, but nature more,
From these our interviews, in which I steal
From all I may be or have been before,
To mingle with the universe, and feel
What I can ne'er express, yet can not all conceal.

George Gordon, Lord Byron

Beyond the horizon's rim

The principal motive of the wander-spirit is curiosity – the desire to know what is beyond the next turning of the road, and to probe for oneself the mystery of the names of the places in maps. In a subconscious way the born wanderer is always expecting to come on something very wonderful – beyond the horizon's rim. The joys of wandering are often balanced by the pains; but there is something which is neither joy nor pain which makes the desire to wander or explore almost incurable in many human beings.

Stephen Graham

Heavy with sunshine

The sun has climbed the hill, the day is on the downward slope.
Between the morning and the afternoon,
   stand I here with my soul, and lift it up.
My soul is heavy with sunshine, and steeped with strength.
The sunbeams have filled me like a honeycomb,
It is the moment of fullness, and the top of the morning.

D.H. Lawrence

Scaling the heights

*Colin Thubron's novel is about five travellers setting out to find
the last city of the Incas deep in the Peruvian Andes.*

All next morning, circled by empty mountains, they wound for
thousands of feet up the wall of the Apurimac valley, until their
track tilted over a watershed to move above cloud-filled ravines.
The going was hard from the start. It wrenched at unaccustomed
muscles and chafed tender skin. But even after four hours'
climbing they were laughing a little, and found the energy to sing
beneath some *chilka* trees where they examined their feet for
blisters. They looked back in wonder across the valley they had
descended yesterday, tracing the hairline of their path where it
wavered down a seeming precipice. A muted pride touched them.
It looked possible only to goats.

Colin Thubron

A sparrow's flight

The present life of men on earth, O king, as compared with the whole length of time which is unknowable to us, seems to me to be like this: as if, when you are sitting at dinner with your chiefs and ministers in wintertime, one of the sparrows from outside flew very quickly through the hall; as if it came in one door and soon went out through another. In that actual time it is indoors it is not touched by the winter's storm; but yet the tiny period of calm is over in a moment, and having come out of the winter it soon returns to the winter and slips out of your sight. Man's life appears to be more or less like this; and of what may follow it, or what preceded it, we are absolutely ignorant.

The Venerable Bede

Beyond comfort zones

We can create a very safe world for ourselves. A world which guards us from risks. A world which shelters us from new challenges. A world where the very fabric of our routines not only sustains us, but also anaesthetizes us.

The inner life cannot fully develop under these circumstances. Safety is not always a key to growth. But questioning, searching and risk-taking are.

Charles Ringma

Running blind

Sometimes 'moving on' may prove to be running away.

I fled him, down the nights and down the days;
I fled him, down the arches of the years;
I fled him, down the labyrinthine ways
Of my own mind; and in the mist of tears
I hid from him, and under running laughter.
    Up vistaed hopes I sped;
    And shot, precipitated,
Adown Titanic glooms of chasmed fears,
From those strong feet that followed, followed after.
    But with unhurrying chase,
    And unperturbèd pace,
Deliberate speed, majestic instancy,
    They beat – and a voice beat
    More instant than the feet –
'All things betray thee, who betrayest me.'

    Halts by me that footfall:
    Is my gloom, after all,
Shade of his hand, outstretched caressingly?
    'Ah, fondest, blindest, weakest,
    I am he whom thou seekest!
Thou dravest love from thee, who dravest me.'

Francis Thompson

No game

Alastair Cameron has often imagined himself as the courageous, conquering young hero in an adventure story. One day he has an odd experience on a train and suddenly real danger threatens — and feels very different.

I had read many adventure stories, and I used to play a game imagining myself to be the hero facing dreadful perils with cool courage. But this was no game, and now that I knew my life to be in danger I was afraid. None of the heroes in my stories was ever afraid. Sword in hand, they fought off half a score of attackers with a smile on their lips. But this was different. A whispered word, spoken in the darkness of the night, could be far more frightening that a dozen sword blades.

Allan McLean

Learning curve

It is striking how every adventure follows the same pattern, develops along the same curve.

There is first an abrupt ascent, explosive, all-powerful, and irresistible. And soon comes a long descent, in which the adventure is exhausted as it is consolidated, in which those who have experienced it try to preserve the treasure of truth and excitement that has thrilled them, but without believing in it any longer with the same boldness or feeling the same joy. This alternation of brief phases of growth with long phases of organization corresponds with the nature of life itself.

Paul Tournier

The journey

This poem speaks of choosing the right road and of the pain that this might involve.

And if you go up that way, you will meet with a man
Leading a horse, whose eyes declare:
There is no God. Take no notice.
There will be other roads and other men
With the same creed, whose lips yet utter
Friendlier greeting, men who have learned
To pack a little of the sun's light
In their cold eyes, whose hands are waiting
For your hand. But do not linger.
A smile is payment; the road runs on
With many turnings towards the tall
Tree to which the believer is nailed.

R.S. Thomas

 **Journeyings**

It is now

Tired
And lonely,
So tired
The heart aches,
Meltwater trickles
Down the rocks,
The fingers are numb,
The knees tremble.
It is now,
Now, that you must not give in.

On the path of the others
Are resting places,
Places in the sun
Where they can meet.
But this
Is your path,
And it is now,
Now, that you must not fail.

Weep
If you can,
Weep,
But do not complain
The way chose you –
And you must be thankful.

Dag Hammarskjöld

Uphill

Does the road wind uphill all the way?
    Yes, to the very end.
Will the day's journey take the whole long day?
    From morn to night, my friend.

But is there for the night a resting place?
    A roof for when the slow dark hours begin.
May not the darkness hide it from my face?
    You cannot miss that inn.

Shall I meet other wayfarers at night?
    Those who have gone before.
Then must I knock, or call when just in sight?
    They will not keep you standing at that door.

Shall I find comfort, travel-sore and weak?
    Of labour you shall find the sum.
Will there be beds for me and all who seek?
    Yea, beds for all who come.

Christina Rossetti

Further up and further in

'You need not mourn over Narnia, Lucy,' said the Lord Digory. 'All of the old Narnia that mattered, all the dear creatures, have been drawn into the real Narnia through the Door. And of course it is different; as different as a real thing is from a shadow or as waking life is from a dream...'

It is as hard to explain how this sunlit land was different from the old Narnia as it would be to tell you how the fruits of that country taste. Perhaps you will get some idea of it if you think like this. You may have been in a room in which there was a window that looked out on a lovely bay of the sea or a green valley that wound away among the mountains. And in the wall of that room opposite to the window there may have been a looking glass. And as you turned away from the window you suddenly caught sight of that sea or that valley, all over again, in the looking glass. And the sea in the mirror, or the valley in the mirror, were in one sense just the same as the real ones: yet at the same time they were somehow different – deeper, more wonderful, more like places in a story: in a story you have never heard but very much want to know. The difference between the old Narnia and the new Narnia was like that.

C.S. Lewis

So near...

The Pied Piper takes all but one of Hamelin's children into a new country. The one left behind speaks of his sadness.

It's dull in our town since my playmates left!
I can't forget that I'm bereft
Of all the pleasant sights they see,
Which the Piper also promised me,
For he led us, he said, to a joyous land,
Joining the town and just at hand,
Where waters gushed and fruit trees grew,
And flowers put forth a fairer hue,
And everything was strange and new;
The sparrows were brighter than peacocks here,
And the dogs outran our fallow deer,
And honeybees had lost their stings,
And horses were born with eagles' wings;
And just as I became assured
My lame foot would be speedily cured,
The music stopped, and I stood still,
And found myself outside the Hill,
Left alone against my will,
To go now limping as before,
And never hear of that country more...

Robert Browning

Journeyings

Home at last!

It was the Unicorn who summed up what everyone was feeling. He stamped his right forehoof on the ground and neighed and then cried: 'I have come home at last! This is my real country! I belong here. This is the land I have been looking for all my life, though I never knew it till now. The reason why we loved the old Narnia is that it sometimes looked a little like this.'

C.S. Lewis

Time line

When as a child I laughed and wept,
Time crept.

When as a youth I dreamed and talked,
Time walked.

When I became a full-grown man,
Time ran.

Thereafter as I older grew,
Time flew.

Soon I shall find, while travelling on,
Time gone.

Will Christ have saved my soul by then?
Amen.

Anon

Arrival

Not conscious
   that you have been seeking
      suddenly
   you come upon it

the village in the Welsh hills
      dust free
   with no road out
but the one you came in by.
      A bird chimes
      from a green tree
the hour that is no hour
   you know. The river dawdles
to hold a mirror for you
where you may see yourself
   as you are, a traveller
   with the moon's halo
   above him, who has arrived
   after long journeying where he
   began, catching this
   one truth by surprise
that there is everything to look forward to.

R.S. Thomas

After the storm

'A life lived in fear is a life half lived,' says Ophelia to her sister. Later, Clementine writes this story to illustrate to a friend how she has been released from crippling anxiety.

Our aim must be to ensure that the strength and meaning which gave beauty to the old patterns is remembered in the pattern now emerging.

Colin Murray Parkes

You remember the little creature who lived her life expecting a catastrophe, how she could never relax and enjoy her beautiful house filled with treasures because she was so frightened of losing it? How she used to stand by her bedroom window in the white and yellow wooden turret looking out at the blue sea, her face all elongated with anxiety; waiting, waiting, always waiting, blind to the sun shining in the blue sky, deaf to the birds singing in her garden.

And what do you know? Finally it happened. The catastrophe she had feared for so long arrived. It was night and the little creature was sleeping her uneasy dream-spun sleep, when she was woken by a sound like a huge train hurtling through a tunnel. Terrified, she leaped from her bed and raced across to the window. Outside the black night was wild and the sea birds were fleeing towards the wood for shelter, their wings battling against the wind. And what a wind. It hurled itself against the lovely house, battering it until there was nothing left but a heap of bricks and sticks of wood, and then, sated, it died down to a soft breeze. Morning came, and never had there been a more beautiful dawn as the sky turned pink and gold in celebration of the rising sun. If you had happened to walk along the seashore, you would have seen the little creature alone among the ruins of her home, dancing, her skinny legs flying, her arms raised towards the sky. You see, she was happy at last. The worst had finally happened, but she had seen the sun rise in the sky and the birds still sang, only now she heard them, and for the first time in her life she was free.

Marika Cobbold

Comings and goings

'And the squirrels have gone,' wailed Nico, 'and the ducks. They've been frightened away... driven away. Why do all the best things go?'

'Oh, but they don't, my dear.' The old lady seemed surprised. 'I loved the fox. He was beautiful and bright. But I knew he killed the chickens. You mustn't think that everything that goes is nice, and everything new is horrid.'

'Most things,' said Jeremy suddenly, 'are a bit nice and a bit horrid.'

The old lady nodded vigorously. 'So you've found that out, have you?' she said.

'Oh, I've known that for ages,' said Jeremy, as if it wasn't important.

Leila Berg

Mixed emotions

When something new is happening in your life, you have to pause to take stock. If you have been trundling along on automatic, you now have to give some thought to what is happening or about to happen. This demands extra energy on top of your usual requirements. You have to decide in what way you need to behave differently, or how you should cope with differences that have been forced upon you. It produces tension and uncertainty: because these changes are new you can't be sure how you will feel or how well you will cope. Your emotions are affected: they can be up one minute with anticipation and down a moment later because of fear of the unknown, or simply because it is natural for an anticlimax to follow excitement.

These conflicting emotions continue throughout the period of adjustment. Volatile emotions take their toll on your energy, and the longer they go on fluctuating the more depleted you will feel. During this period of adjustment your daily routines may be changing and you may need to come to terms with new ways of doing things. The conscious mental effort involved is exhausting.

After a while everything settles down. The new becomes normal and the extra effort goes out of your daily life. Even so, it is not quite over: now you need a period of recuperation to replenish your energies.

Embracing the variables

Douglas was a good engineer. He had always been good at the sums. He sat at his desk with the surveyor's figures, doing the site plans and working out the specifications. The plans for the Bent Bridge were rolled up in his hand now.

Out on site, you were never parted from your plans. They were your Bible. They got dog-eared, yellowed, smeared with mud, peppered with little holes from where you had unrolled them on the ground.

But although so sacred, the plans were only the start. Once you got out there on the site everything was different. No matter how carefully done, the plans could not foresee the *variables*. It was always interesting, this moment when you saw for the first time the actual site rather than the idealized drawings of it.

He knew men who hated the *variables*. They had their plans and by golly they were going to stick to them. If the site did not match the drawings it was like a personal insult.

He himself liked the variables best. He liked the way that the solution to one problem created another problem further down the line, so that you had to think up something else, and that in turn created another problem to solve. It was an exchange, backwards and forwards. Some men thought of it as a war, but to him it was more like a conversation.

Kate Grenville

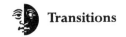
In the beginning

Life is full of beginnings. They occur every day and every hour to every person. Most beginnings are small and appear trivial and insignificant, but in reality they are the most important things in life.

See how in the material world everything proceeds from small beginnings. The mightiest river is at first a rivulet over which the grasshopper could leap; the great flood commences with a few drops of rain; the sturdy oak, that has endured the storms of a thousand winters, was once an acorn.

Consider how in the spiritual world the greatest things proceed from the smallest beginnings. A light fancy may be the inception of a wonderful invention or an immortal work of art; a spoken sentence may turn the tide of history; a pure thought entertained may lead to the exercise of a worldwide regenerative power.

There are right beginnings and wrong beginnings, followed by effects of like nature.

Loving, gentle, kind, unselfish and pure thoughts are right beginnings.

James Allen

Anticlimax

*Katie is married to David, a cynical, angry man. He has just
told her that he isn't angry any more.*

I sigh, heavily.

'I thought you'd be pleased.'

I thought I would be pleased, too. If, a few weeks ago,
someone had offered to grant me one wish, I think I would
probably have chosen to wish for exactly this, because I would
not have been able to think of anything else, not even money,
that could have improved the quality of my life – our lives – so
dramatically. And I would have said, after a great deal of thought,
'I would like David not to be angry any more. I would like him
to recognize that his life is OK, that his children are wonderful,
that he has a loyal and loving and a not unattractive or unintelligent
wife, and enough money for babysitters and meals out and the
mortgage… I would like all his bile gone, every inch, or ounce,
or millilitre of it.' And the genie would have rubbed his stomach,
and hey presto! David is a happy person.

And, hey presto! David is a happy person, or at least a calm
person, here, now, in the real world, and all I do is sigh. The
thing is, of course, I don't really want the hey presto! part. I am
a rationalist, and I don't believe in genies, or sudden personality
changes. I wanted David's anger to vanish only after years and
years in therapy.

Nick Hornby

Wouldn't it be lovely?

*Four women impulsively take a holiday in a castle on the Italian
Riviera – a decision that has life-changing consequences. Here
the author describes the seemingly unimportant incident that
triggers off this chain of events.*

It began in a woman's club in London on a February afternoon
– an uncomfortable club, and a miserable afternoon – when Mrs
Wilkins, who had come down from Hampstead to shop and had
lunched at her club, took up *The Times* from the table in the
smoking room, and running her listless eye down the Agony
Column saw this:

> To Those who Appreciate Wistaria and Sunshine. Small medieval
> Italian Castle on the shores of the Mediterranean to be Let
> Furnished for the month of April. Necessary servants remain.
> Z, Box 1000, *The Times*.

*Observing that Mrs Arbuthnot, a woman she only knows by sight,
has noticed the same advertisement, Mrs Wilkins initiates a crucial
conversation.*

'Wouldn't it be wonderful?' murmured Mrs Wilkins.
    'Wonderful,' said Mrs Arbuthnot. Her face, which had lit up,
faded into patience again. 'Very wonderful,' she said. 'But it's no
use wasting one's time thinking of such things.'

'Oh, but it *is*,' was Mrs Wilkins' quick, surprising reply. 'And just the considering of them is worthwhile in itself – such a change from Hampstead – and sometimes I believe – I really do believe – if one considers hard enough one gets things.'

Elizabeth Von Arnim

Lesson plan

You say you are chained by circumstances; you cry out for better opportunities, for a wider scope, for improved physical conditions, and perhaps you inwardly curse the fate that binds you hand and foot. You may bring about that improved condition in your outward life which you desire if you will unswervingly resolve to improve your inner life.

Be sure, first of all, that you are making the best of what you have. Do not delude yourself into supposing that you can step into greater advantages whilst overlooking smaller ones, for if you could, the advantage would be impermanent and you would quickly fall back again in order to learn the lesson which you had neglected. As the child at school must master one standard before passing on to the next, so, before you can have that greater good which you so desire, must you faithfully employ that which you already possess.

James Allen

As time goes by

And so it went on: growing up, growing happier, taking good turnings and bad ones, marrying, having children, rusticating, being a working mother and all the rest of it. This is not a book about a career, but about growing up; so the narrative, I think, should more or less stop right here. The last part of this book will become far more general, far more objective. Which feels right, because, quite frankly, even in an age of non-stop therapy for all, it befits adults to be more objective and less obsessed with their own development than adolescents and children. It is a quarter of a century now since I began, tentatively, to consider myself more or less grown-up; of course there are changes and miniature conversions, and always will be, but by the time you are twenty-five the important foundations of thought and belief are laid down. Their outlines will show through every action until death; and, no doubt, beyond it.

So the rest can go unchronicled for the moment. There is no space here – nor would it be kind or decorous – to give a blow-by-blow account of a media career, still less of marriage and childbearing. This is no time to chart the slow comfortable wearing-down of those sharp early passions into the pragmatic dogged kindnesses of family life and the jerky, uneven slog of earning a freelance living. It is far more fun, anyway, to express these things in novels.

Older and wiser

*String Lug the Fox, the hero of David Stephen's story, notices
a change and learns from it.*

String Lug did not jump onto the boulder. He wanted first of all
to investigate the matter of its changed appearance. Wading out
to it, shoulder deep, he sniffed critically. Through the odour of
the moss, and in spite of the scent-destroying wash of water, he
recognized the smell... Steel! String Lug pondered, but did not
paw. He gripped the outer fuzz of the moss covering and jerked,
sliding back on his haunches till he almost fell in the water. The
gin lay exposed, slick on his stepping-stone, with jaws spread to
catch his feet.

At that moment String Lug knew fear – real fear. It is doubtful
if he realized at once that the gin had been set specially for
himself. What he did appreciate was that he might well have
walked right into it had he not stopped to consider the boulder's
altered appearance. But when he found another gin carefully
planted beside his favourite rowan tree on the ridge, he knew
that it was meant for him. And that was the beginning of trap
wisdom for String Lug.

David Stephen

A fighting spirit

*Little Henry Pratt is asking his Auntie Kate about something that
has troubled him ever since the days when he shared a bedroom
with his parents, who have both since died.*

'Auntie Kate?'

His solemnity was comical. He spoke with the air of someone
who has thought long and hard about a subject of deep importance,
as indeed he had. But she had herself under control. She wouldn't
laugh at him now.

'Aye. What is it?'

'I saw me dad on top of me mam doing summat that weren't
strangling, and I don't know what it were, and when I asked me
mam she were right cagey about it. Does tha know what they
were doing, Auntie Kate?'

Auntie Kate didn't reply. She was leaning on the window sill
and shaking.

'Only I thought tha might know what it were 'cos I thought
happen Uncle Frank might have tried it with thee,' said Henry.

Auntie Kate threw back her head and roared with laughter.
She went bright red with mirth.

Henry went red too. The shame of being laughed at and by
Auntie Kate of all people was too much. The terrible hot shame
of it.

Auntie Kate stopped laughing.

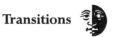

'I'm sorry,' she said.

And then, the unexpected happened. Henry Pratt, frightened of being laughed at, frightened of his own father, frightened of falling into water, frightened of railway engines, frightened of children, and frightened of being ejected from wombs, discovered that he had a fighting spirit.

'It's not fair to laugh at me because I don't know things,' he said. 'I can't know everything. I'm only little.'

David Nobbs

A place to grow

If there is not a place where tears are understood,
Where can I go to cry?

If there is not a place where my spirit can take wing,
Where do I go to fly?

If there is not a place where my questions can be asked,
Where do I go to seek?

If there is not a place where my feelings can be heard,
Where do I go to speak?

If there is not a place where I can try and learn and grow,
Where can I just be me?

Anon

Loss adjustments

Everyone knows that when someone you love dies you mourn. It is less well understood that you can also mourn and feel grief when major changes happen in your life. You can grieve for the loss of 'your old self' or for a relationship that has finished or for a relationship that has changed so much that it is now different. You can also grieve for places that you have left for good: a family home or the town in which you always lived. You can grieve for lost jobs or for your children's childhood as they grow into adults. Obviously some of these happenings are much less painful and you go through the grieving stages quite quickly, but if you know that this is natural you might be able to better understand what is happening to you. These are the classic stages:

Shock. Obvious symptoms of this stage are not being able to think straight, repeating yourself and forgetting things.

Yearning. You want back what you have lost. You feel anger and sadness and periods of disbelief. You may feel very restless and on edge, full of useless energy.

Depression. As you come to terms with what you have lost you become depressed and apathetic. The energy goes and you can't feel much about anything.

Recovery. You start to adapt to your loss. You stop living in the past and begin to reorganize your life under the new conditions.

Sarah Litvinoff

Fully present

My difficulty is that on the whole I am not very good at change; I cling to the safe and the known. Caught up in the miseries and the confusions of what I am losing, I find I am unwilling to believe that new life is anything more than a distant promise. As my sons leave home and the house becomes emptier, I do them and myself only a disservice by clinging to fond memories of times when large numbers gathered round the family table. I must let them go in freedom, both for their own sakes and for mine, and I must try to turn this newly found space in my life to good account and not simply fill it with busyness to cover up the void. I must live in this moment, not looking either forward or back, or to right or left, but realizing that unless I am what I am there cannot be any growth. If I promise myself that life will be better, that I shall be a more agreeable person, that I shall be closer to God on the next stage along the way, then I am failing to live as I am called to live, because I go on dreaming of that ideal which does not exist. The past has brought me to this moment, and if I begin today anew I can also begin tomorrow anew and the day after that, and so I shall be truly open to change.

Esther de Waal

A losing battle?

Felicity had sent away to Sydney for a new book that had diagrams of chin-tightening exercises. You started by pulling the mouth out sideways into a kind of leer. Then you tensed the muscles around your neck and jaw. She tried it in front of the bathroom mirror. It was rather grotesque.

However, she could see how it exercised all the muscles that held up your chin. They stood out in a frill of tendons around your jaw.

It was probably very good for you, even though it did make you look as if you were being electrocuted.

She did it six times, and then the muscles began to ache. *No pain, no gain.* That was what the books said. So she did seven more.

Hugh said he did not care, and he probably meant it. *Darling, I'd love you even with wrinkles*, he had told her, many times. She thought it was probably true. He was not one of those men who would trade in their wife once she got old, and replace her with something that had no *laugh-lines*. Hugh was a man who liked life to stay the same. She thought he had made a sort of agreement with life, that he would not demand too much of it, if it left him alone.

It was nothing to do with Hugh, the staving-off of the laugh-lines and so on.

It was something more private than that, and more important.

She did another chin-clench in the mirror. The trouble was that although making yourself look electrocuted tightened up the muscles around your chin, it also creased the whole of the lower part of your face up into *lines*.

The question was, whether the *chin-firming* effect was enough to make up for the *line-forming* effect. It was yet another little dilemma.

You had to fight the feeling, sometimes, that your body had a mind of its own. But a person could not be on guard forever against themselves.

Kate Grenville

Not

Thick around
the middle,
not fat.
Receding,
not going bald.
Tired eyes,
not failing sight.
Maturing features,
not wrinkled skin.
Growing older,
not dying.

Steve Turner

Inner glow

Antonia came in and stood before me; a stalwart, brown woman, flat-chested, her curly brown hair a little grizzled. It was a shock, of course. It always is, to meet people after long years, especially if they have lived as much and as hard as this woman had. We stood looking at each other. The eyes that peered anxiously at me were – simply Antonia's eyes. I had seen no others like them since I looked into them last, though I had looked at so many thousands of human faces. As I confronted her, the changes grew less apparent to me, her identity stronger. She was there, in the full vigour of her personality, battered but not diminished, looking at me, speaking to me in that husky, breathy voice I remembered so well…

I was thinking, as I watched her, how little it mattered – about her teeth, for instance. I know so many women who have kept all the things that she had lost, but whose inner glow has faded. Whatever else was gone, Antonia had not lost the fire of life. Her skin, so brown and hardened, had not that look of flabbiness, as if the sap beneath it had been secretly drawn away.

Willa Cather

Wide open

I was born for seeing,
I am employed to watch,
I am bound by my oath to this tower,
and I love the world.
I look into the distance
and see, as from nearby,
the moon and the stars,
the forest and the deer.
And in all of them I see
the eternal adornment;
and as the world delights me,
so I delight myself.
Oh, happy eyes,
whatever you have seen,
let it be as it may be,
it has been so beautiful!

Johann Wolfgang von Goethe

Transformations

What a wonderful world!

God gave us a world unfinished, so that we might share in the joys and satisfactions of creation.

He left oil in Trenton rock; he left electricity in the clouds; he left the rivers unbridged – and the mountains untrailed; he left the forests unfelled and the cities unbuilt; he left the laboratories unopened; he left the diamonds uncut; he gave us the challenge of raw materials, not the satisfaction of perfect, finished things; he left the music unsung and the dramas unplayed; he left the poetry undreamed: in order that men and women might not become bored, but engage in stimulating, exciting, creative activities that keep them thinking, working, experimenting and experiencing all the joys and durable satisfactions of achievement.

Allen A. Stockdale

It gets better

The stars were wonderful enough in all conscience when we thought of them as lamps of light set in a solid sky to guide the sailors on their journey over the trackless sea; but they are a million times more wonderful now that we know them to be blazing worlds that move through the vast infinities of space in accordance with exact mathematical laws.

Our own bodies were wonderful enough when we thought of them as created in a moment by the fiat of the Almighty from the dust of the earth; but how much more wonderful they have become since the sciences of physiology and embryology have taught us to trace their growth through countless stages from the humblest kind of beginning to their present complex end.

G.A. Studdert-Kennedy

Wondrous sweetness

A Persian fable says: One day
A wanderer found a piece of clay,
So redolent of sweet perfume
Its odour scented all the room.
'What art thou?' was the quick demand;
'Art thou some gem of Samarkand?
Or spikenard rare in rich disguise,
Or other costly merchandise?'
'Nay, I am but a piece of clay.'
'Then whence this wondrous sweetness, pray?'
'Friend, if the secret I disclose,
I have been dwelling with the rose.'

Anon

Beautiful changes

We are inclined to make life heavy and see only what must be done, not what could be done. We let the evening news take away our delight in the beauty of a sunset. The ugly becomes more real than the good.

The worst thing in the world is to believe that today is exactly like yesterday. Then we forget to notice and to share what is new and fresh and good about today. What is worse, as we grow older, we have difficulty stretching our minds to connect what may be small, delightful and everyday with what is big, eternal and true. Without this we become spectators of life, not feeling much, not expecting much, and always playing it safe. Truth and joy become the security of bank accounts, instead of a sunrise or a bird's nest or a beautiful story.

Gladys Hunt

I can understand the complex process of keratin producing rigid fingernails and horses' hooves. But no amount of training will lessen my astonishment as I watch a single stalk of keratin push its way out of a follicle, grow erect and proud and shockingly unfurl as a peacock feather. What was chemistry becomes beauty. It is as if a brilliant Appalachian quilt springs from a rock, as if a desert suddenly births a gang of cavorting porpoises.

Paul Brand and Philip Yancey

No comment

Triumphantly the chemist
drips the embryo
from the test tube.
The world gazes in awe.
SIGNIFICANT ACHIEVEMENT
AMAZING STEP FORWARD
yell the banner headlines.

Outside in the lush grasses
and wilderness gardens
God bursts a thousand seed pods
and floats a billion thistledowns
upon the breezes.
Broom, rape, gutweed,
bladderwrack, balm.
Each seed individual
unique recognizable created
expelled into life
daily hourly around the world.

And we make no comment,
no comment at all.

Sylvia Mandeville

Healing

What if pain does not go,
What then? Scars can be
Touched to raw response in
Unexpected moments
Long after the event which
Caused them, nerve ends twitch
Perhaps forever after
Amputation.

Healing is not achieved
Without some cost. It
May not mean the end of
Pain. Healing can hurt
Just like fresh wounds,
As pockets of poison are
Lanced, or lesions cut to
Allow more flexibility. For
Healing is not going back
To what one was before,
It is a growing on
To a new stage of being,
Through many deaths and
Resurrections being set free.

Ann Lewin

Making good

Anne Coleman's daughter was murdered and her son took his own life. As a result of this double tragedy, Anne met Barbara Lewis, whose son was on death row. Anne then visited and counselled others there.

That's how I met Billy. He'd had no visitors, and he was very lonely. I cry when I think of how he was hanged; how they made him stand on the gallows in that howling wind for at least fifteen minutes while they waited for the witnesses to arrive. After his execution I thought I couldn't go on.

Then I got to know a little boy called Marcus. His father is also on death row. He has no mother and has lost both of his sisters, and he has nightmares because now he's going to lose his father too.

I know that hating someone is not going to bring my daughter back. And at this point, I don't know if I'll ever find the person who killed her, anyway. But one has to find healing somehow, and I've found it by helping the Barbaras and Marcuses of this world. Helping them has given me more healing than I ever imagined.

Johann Christoph Arnold

Frames of reference

Jeremy discusses various outlooks on life.

In Bernard's company, I always sensed there was an element missing from his account of the world, and that it was June who held the key. The assurance of his scepticism, his invincible atheism made me wary; it was too arrogant, too much was closed off, too much denied. In conversations with June, I found myself thinking like Bernard; I felt stifled by her expressions of faith, and bothered by the unstated assumption of all believers that they are good because they believe what they believe, that faith is virtue, and, by extension, unbelief is unworthy or, at best, pitiable.

Bernard and June often talked to me about ideas that could never sit side by side. Bernard, for example, was certain that there was no direction, no patterning in human affairs or fates other than that which was imposed by human minds. June could not accept this; life had a purpose and it was in our interests to open ourselves to it. Nor will it do to suggest that both these views are correct. To believe everything, to make no choices, amounts to much the same thing, to my mind, as believing in nothing at all. But I would be false to my own experience if I did not declare my belief in the possibility of love transforming and redeeming a life.

Ian McEwan

Faith

Spring is a promise
in the closed fist
of a long winter. All
we have got is a raw
slant of light at a low
angle, a rising river
of wind, and an icy rain
that drowns out green
in a tide of mud. It is
the daily postponement
that disillusions. (Once
again the performance
has been cancelled by
the management.) We live
on legends of old
springs. Each evening
brings only remote
possibilities of
renewal: 'Maybe
tomorrow.' But the
evening and the morning
are the umpteenth day
and the God of sunlit
Eden still looks
on the weather
and calls it good.

Luci Shaw

113

Love's alchemy

Every now and then Scrap's eyes lingered on Rose; so did Lotty's. For Rose was lovely.

Lotty bent close to Scrap's ear, and whispered. 'Love,' she whispered.

Scrap nodded. 'Yes,' she said, under her breath.

She was obliged to admit it. You only had to look at Rose to know that here was Love.

'It's a great thing,' whispered Lotty after a pause, during which they both watched Rose's upturned face, 'to get on with one's loving. Perhaps you can tell me of anything else in the world that works such wonders.'

But Scrap couldn't tell her.

She pulled her wrap closer round her with a gesture of defence. She didn't want to grow sentimental. Difficult not to, here; the marvellous night stole in through all one's chinks, and brought in with it, whether one wanted them or not, enormous feelings, at once rapture and terror and immense, heart-cleaving longing.

'I suppose,' whispered Lotty, 'Rose's husband seems to you just an ordinary, good-natured, middle-aged man... He isn't. Rose sees through all that. That's mere trimmings. She sees what we can't see, because she loves him.'

Elizabeth Von Arnim

Prayer to the alchemist

I pray you
take this weeping heart
and all the broken thing
that lies within your hand.
Distil the agony
until
from all its hurt
a single drop of sweetness
may remain
changing the substance
of this death in earth
to make all new –
a rising sap
to bring the transformation
of the spring.

Margaret Torrie

Open house

Braving reprisals from the government and the Nazi SS, the people of Le Chambon saved the lives of thousands of Jews. Thirty-six years later, Magda Trocme, the vicar's wife, tells Philip Hallie:

'A German woman knocked at my door. It was in the evening, and she said she was a German Jew, coming from northern France, that she was in danger, and that she had heard that in Le Chambon somebody could help her. Could she come into my house? I said, "Naturally, come in, and come in." Lots of snow. She had a little pair of shoes, nothing.'

If we would understand the goodness that happened in Le Chambon, we must see how easy it was for them to refuse to give up their consciences, to refuse to participate in hatred, betrayal and murder, and to help the desperate adults and the terrified children who knocked on their doors in Le Chambon. We must see this, and we must also see the many elements that came together to make these things happen. Goodness is the simplest thing in the world, and the most complex.

I know what I want to have the power to be. I know that I want to have a door in the depths of my being, a door that is not locked against the faces of all other human beings. I know that I want to say, from those depths, 'Naturally, come in, and come in.'

Philip Hallie

Angel unawares

Rachel Lane is a young woman who has chosen to be a missionary in the Brazilian jungle. Nate O'Riley's job is to find her and tell her that she has been left a fortune. Nate, an alcoholic whose life is in a mess, finds in Rachel the catalyst for change. Then she dies of malaria.

Buried there was Rachel Lane, the bravest person Nate had ever known because she had absolutely no fear of death. She welcomed it. She was at peace, her soul finally with the Lord, her body forever lying among the people she loved.

He knew her well enough to know she wouldn't want anyone grieving. She wouldn't approve of tears, and Nate had none to give her. For a few moments he stared at her grave in disbelief, but reality soon set in. This was not an old friend with whom he'd shared many moments. He'd barely known her. His motives in finding her had been purely selfish. He had invaded her privacy, and she had asked him not to return.

But his heart ached anyway. He'd thought about her every day since he'd left the Pantanal. He'd dreamed of her, felt her touch, heard her voice, remembered her wisdom. She had taught him to pray, and given him hope. She was the first person in decades to see anything good in him.

He had never met anyone like Rachel Lane, and he missed her greatly.

John Grisham

Getting a life

After Bertram's sudden death, Flora realizes that, having lived in her husband's shadow, she now needs to make her own decisions. Here she is talking to an acquaintance about her plans.

Mrs Carpenter leaned forward a little, towards the fire.

'I will not give way to old age and death,' she said in a firm voice. 'I will not go into a decline and live off the kindness of others, because I am now a widow. No, I have quite decided to take myself in hand *at once*. I shall fill my life very full, Miss Prug; it is the only way to help me bear the loss of my husband. I shall have my own flat and my own furniture about me and I shall start to live a social life again, entertain my friends and have guests to stay. But I do not want to spend every day looking for ways of passing the time and diverting myself, so I have decided to find a little voluntary work, perhaps do something with the hospital, you know, or children's charities. I have not yet looked into it fully. But I am a rich woman, after all, and there must be a great deal for me to do.'

Susan Hill

Taking the plunge

A sufferer from eating disorders, Ellie comes to realize that she can take control of her life – and stand up to others.

I go downstairs for my coffee. I have one of Anna's home-made cookies too, savouring every mouthful. I'm scared I'll want another and another, eating until I've emptied the tin.

No. I don't have to binge. I don't have to starve. I don't want to end up one of those sad sick girls in Zoe's ward. I'm going to eat what I want, when I want. I can do it. I *can*.

I put my swimming costume on under my school uniform and grab a towel. Anna is in the kitchen buttering rolls.

'I don't want breakfast, Anna.'

'What?' She looks stricken.

'Only because I'm going swimming. I'll take a roll with me and eat it after, OK?'

'OK,' says Anna.

I don't know if she totally trusts me. I'm not even sure I trust myself. I stride out towards the swimming pool, but as I get nearer I start to feel sick. There's every chance Mick and his mates will be there… I'm shivering now. I must be mad. I *can't* go swimming.

I can, I can, I can.

Jacqueline Wilson

Coup de grâce

Embittered ex-convict Jean Valjean accepts hospitality from a bishop. During the night, he gets up, steals his host's silver cutlery and runs away. But the police catch him and bring him back. What happens next changes Valjean forever.

'So, here you are!' the bishop cried to Valjean. 'I'm delighted to see you. Have you forgotten that I gave you the candlesticks as well?'

'You mean,' said the sergeant, 'that we can let him go?'

'Certainly.'

The gendarmes released Valjean and withdrew.

'But this time,' said the bishop, 'you must not forget your candlesticks.'

He fetched them from the mantelpiece and handed them to Valjean. Valjean stayed motionless, as though he were on the verge of collapse. The bishop came up to him and said in a low voice:

'Do not forget, do not ever forget that you have promised me to use the money to make yourself an honest man.'

Valjean, who did not recall having made any promise, was silent. The bishop had spoken the words slowly and deliberately. He concluded with solemn emphasis:

'Jean Valjean, my brother, you no longer belong to what is evil but to what is good. I have bought your soul to save it from black thoughts and the spirit of perdition, and I give it to God.'

Victor Hugo

Homecoming

There was a man who had two sons. The younger one said to his father, 'Father, give me my share of the estate.' So he divided his property between them.

Not long after that, the younger son got together all he had, set off for a distant country and there squandered his wealth in wild living. After he had spent everything, there was a severe famine in that whole country, and he began to be in need. So he went and hired himself out to a citizen of that country, who sent him to his fields to feed pigs. He longed to fill his stomach with the pods that the pigs were eating, but no one gave him anything.

When he came to his senses, he said, 'How many of my father's hired men have food to spare, and here I am starving to death! I will set out and go back to my father and say to him: "Father, I have sinned against heaven and against you. I am no longer worthy to be called your son; make me like one of your hired men."' So he got up and went to his father.

But while he was still a long way off, his father saw him and was filled with compassion for him; he ran to his son, threw his arms around him and kissed him. He said to his servants, 'Quick! Bring the best robe and put it on him. Put a ring on his finger and sandals on his feet. Let's have a feast and celebrate. For this son of mine was dead and is alive again; he was lost and is found.'

The Bible (Luke 15:11–24)

Making amends

Ian's careless words bring about the death of his brother, and of his sister-in-law Lucy. He responds by devoting his life to bringing up Lucy's children, and is finally able to imagine the following exchange.

'I'd like you to meet the woman who's changed my life,' Ian said. His face was very solemn, but Lucy was smiling. 'Your what?' she seemed to be saying. 'Your, what was that? Oh, your *life*.' And she tipped her head and smiled. After all, she might have said, this was an ordinary occurrence. People changed other people's lives every day of the year. There was no call to make such a fuss about it.

Anne Tyler

Listen to your life

If I were called to state in a few words the essence of everything I was trying to say both as a novelist and a preacher, it would be something like this: Listen to your life. See it for the fathomless mystery it is. In the boredom and pain of it no less than in the excitement and gladness: touch, taste, smell your way to the heavenly and hidden heart of it, because in the last analysis all moments are key moments, and life itself is grace.

Frederick Buechner

Love

Love bade me welcome; yet my soul drew back,
    Guilty of dust and sin.
But quick-eyed Love, observing me grow slack
    From my first entrance in,
Drew nearer to me, sweetly questioning
    If I lacked anything.

'A guest,' I answered, 'worthy to be here.'
    Love said, 'You shall be he.'
'I, the unkind, ungrateful? Ah my dear,
    I cannot look on thee.'
Love took my hand, and smiling did reply,
    'Who made the eyes but I?'

'Truth Lord, but I have marred them; let my shame
    Go where it doth deserve.'
'And know you not,' says Love, 'who bore the blame?'
    'My dear, then I will serve.'
'You must sit down,' says Love, 'and taste my meat.'
    So I did sit and eat.

George Herbert

Creative thinking

Due to my involvement in the struggle for the freedom of my people, I have known very few quiet days in the last few years. I have been arrested five times and put in Alabama jails. My home has been bombed twice. A day seldom passes that my family and I are not the recipients of threats of death. I have been the victim of a near-fatal stabbing. So in a real sense I have been battered by the storms of persecution. I must admit that at times I have felt that I could no longer bear such a heavy burden, and have been tempted to retreat to a more quiet and serene life. But every time such a temptation appeared, something came to strengthen and sustain my determination. I have learned now that the Master's burden is light precisely when we take his yoke upon us.

My personal trials have also taught me the value of unmerited suffering. As my sufferings mounted, I soon realized that there were two ways that I could respond to my situation: either to react with bitterness or to seek to transform the suffering into a creative force. Recognizing the necessity for suffering, I have tried to make of it a virtue. If only to save myself from bitterness, I have attempted to see my personal ordeals as an opportunity to transform myself and heal the people involved in the tragic situation which now obtains. I have lived these last few years with the conviction that unearned suffering is redemptive.

An invisible host

May every soul that touches mine —
Be it the slightest contact —
Get therefrom some good;
Some little grace; one kindly thought;
One aspiration yet unfelt;
One bit of courage
For the darkening sky;
One gleam of faith
To brave the thickening ills of life;
One glimpse of brighter skies
Beyond the gathering mists —
To make this life worthwhile
And heaven a surer heritage.

George Eliot

In peace as in war, we are beneficiaries of knowledge contributed by every nation in the world. Our children are guarded from diphtheria by what a Japanese and a German did; they are protected from smallpox by the work of an Englishman; they are saved from rabies because of a Frenchman; they are cured of pellagra through the researches of an Austrian. From birth to death we are surrounded by an invisible host — the spirits of men who never thought in terms of flags or boundary lines and who never served a lesser loyalty than the welfare of mankind.

Raymond B. Fosdick

Everything changes

Everything changes. We plant
trees for those born later
but what's happened has happened,
and poisons poured into the seas
cannot be drained out again.

What's happened has happened.
Poisons poured into the seas
cannot be drained out again, but
everything changes. We plant
trees for those born later.

Cicely Herbert

New day

'Tomorrow the adventure begins anew,' Hodgkins continued.

'Not tomorrow, tonight!' shouted Moomintroll. And in the
foggy dawn they all tumbled out into the garden. The eastern sky
was a wonderful rose-petal pink, promising a fine, clear August
day.

A new door to the Unbelievable, to the Possible, a new day
that can always bring you anything if you have no objection to it.

Tove Jansson

The release

He was released yesterday early.
We were not expecting it to be so soon.
There was no one there to greet him.

When we did meet up
his suit was limp and crumpled
just taken from a long-packed case.
Slowly the fresh air and the gentle breezes
eased the creases from the
soft velvet, glowing in the sunlight:
rich cream and orange brown, vibrantly patterned.

Back in July, the day he went inside,
he had been wearing hairy tweed.
'Woolly Bear' we'd called him.
Today, well tailored,
he edged up the stem from his cocoon
and flew away.

Sylvia Mandeville

 **Acknowledgments**

6: Anne Tyler, *Saint Maybe* (Vintage). 7: from 'In my seventieth year', Kathleen Raine, *Collected Poems 1935–1978* (Allen & Unwin, 1981). 8: Lewis Thomas, *The Medusa and the Snail* (Penguin, 1981) and *The Lives of a Cell* (Penguin, 1980). 10: Rachel Vail, *Wonder* (Heinemann). 11: Dietrich Bonhoeffer, *Letters and Papers from Prison* (Macmillan, 1962). 12: Silvia Rodgers, *Red Saint, Pink Daughter* (Andre Deutsch). 13: Margaret J. Wheatley, *Turning to One Another* (Berrett-Koehler Publishers). 15: Bette Paul, *Breaking the Ties* (Scholastic Ltd). 16: Martha Cooley, *The Archivist* (Abacus). 17: Geraldine Sheridan & Thomas Kenning, *Survivors* (Pan). 18: Kathy Galloway, *Love Burning Deep* (SPCK). Used by permission of the publisher. 21: Elaine Storkey, *The Search for Intimacy* (Hodder & Stoughton). 22: Dick Keyes, *Beyond Identity* (Servant Publications). 23: Marjorie Williams, *The Velveteen Rabbit* (Heinemann). 24: Rosie Rushton, *Tell Me I'm OK, Really* (Piccadilly). 25: A.R. Ammons, *Tape for the Turn of the Year* (W.W. Norton & Company, 1965). 26: from *100 Contemporary Christian Poets*, compiled Gordon Bailey (Lion Publishing). 27: Dick Keyes, *Beyond Identity* (Servant Publications). 28: Brent Curtis & John Eldredge, *The Sacred Romance* (Thomas Nelson). 29: Anne Tyler, *A Patchwork Planet* (Vintage). 30: Brent Curtis & John Eldredge, *The Sacred Romance* (Thomas Nelson). 31: Ursula Hegi, *Stones from the River* (Simon & Schuster). 32: Marika Cobbold, *The Purveyor of Enchantment* (Black Swan). 33: Brent Curtis & John Eldredge, *The Sacred Romance* (Thomas Nelson). 33: Madeleine L'Engle, *Walking on Water* (Lion Publishing). 34: Gladys Hunt, *Honey for a Child's Heart* (Zondervan). 36: Paul Tournier, *The Adventure of Living* (Highland Books). 36: Paulo Freire, *Pedagogy of the Oppressed* (Penguin, 1996), copyright © Paulo Freire, 1970, 1993. Used by permission of the publisher. 38: Peter Kreeft, *Making Sense out of Suffering* (Hodder & Stoughton). 41: Robert Fulghum, *All I Really Needed to Know I Learned in Kindergarten* (HarperCollins). 42: from *Jokes, Quotes and Oneliners for Public Speakers*, Henry V. Prochnow & Herbert V Prochnow Jr (Thorsons). 44: Imogen Parker, *Perfect Day* (Black Swan). 46: Maya Angelou, *The Heart of a Woman* (Virago). 47: from *100 Contemporary Christian Poets*, compiled Gordon Bailey (Lion Publishing). 47: Henri Nouwen, *Reaching Out* (HarperCollins). 48: Nick Hornby, *About a Boy* (Penguin). 49: from *100 Contemporary Christian Poets*, compiled Gordon Bailey (Lion Publishing). 49: Elaine Storkey, *The Search for Intimacy* (Hodder & Stoughton). 50: C.S. Lewis, *The Four Loves* (HarperCollins). 50: Jim Cotter, *Healing – More or Less* (Cairns Publications, 1990). Used by permission of the author. 51: Nick Hornby, *High Fidelity* (Penguin). 52: Helen Keller, *The Story of My Life* (Hodder & Stoughton). 54: John Gray, *Men are from Mars, Women are from Venus* (Thorsons). 55: Olivia Manning, *The Doves of Venus* (Heinemann). 56: Tony Parsons, *One for My Baby* (HarperCollins). 57: Michael Mayne, *This Sunrise of Wonder* (HarperCollins). 58: Albert Schweitzer, *Memoirs of Childhood and Youth* (Syracuse Press). 59: Anne Tyler, *A Patchwork Planet* (Vintage). 60: Barbara Kingsolver, *Pigs in Heaven* (Faber & Faber). 63: John McGahern, *Amongst Women* (Faber & Faber). 66: Laurie Lee, *As I Walked Out One Midsummer May Morning* (Penguin). 67: Patrick Hobbs, *Paper Hands* (Dancing Blue Press, 2001). Used by permission of the author. 67: Fleur Adcock, *Poems 1960–2000* (Bloodaxe Books, 2000). Used by permission of the publisher. 68: Ann Holm, *I Am David* (Mammoth). 69: Ken Smith, *Shed: Poems 1980–2001* (Bloodaxe Books, 2002). Used by permission of the publisher. 70: Madge Jenison, 'About Roads' in *The Magic of Walking*, Aaron Sussman & Ruth Goode (Simon & Schuster). 72: John Bunyan, *Pilgrim's Progress* (Penguin). 73: Dale & Juanita Ryan, *Rooted in God's Love* (IVP). 75: John Eldredge, *The Journey of Desire* (Thomas Nelson). 76: Stephen Graham, 'The Gentle Art of Tramping' in *The Magic of Walking*, Aaron Sussman & Ruth Goode (Simon & Schuster). 77: Colin Thubron, *To the Last City* (Chatto & Windus). 78: Charles Ringma, *Dare to Journey* (Albatross). 79: Francis Thompson, 'The Hound of Heaven'. 80: Allan McLean, *The Hill of the Red Fox* (HarperCollins). 80: Paul Tournier, *The Adventure of Living* (Highland Books). 81: R.S. Thomas, *Selected Poems 1946–1968* (Bloodaxe Books, 1986). Used by permission of the publisher. 82: from *The Pain Bearers*, Ann Bird, © Trustees for Methodist Church Purposes. Used by permission of Methodist Publishing House. 84: C.S. Lewis, *The Last Battle* (HarperCollins). 86: C.S. Lewis, *The Last Battle* (HarperCollins). 87: R.S. Thomas, *Selected Poems 1946–1968* (Bloodaxe Books, 1986). Used by permission of the publisher. 88: Marika Cobbold, *The Purveyor of Enchantment* (Black Swan). 89: Leila Berg, *The Hidden Road* (Hamish Hamilton). 90: Sarah Litvinoff, *The Relate Guide to Better Relationships* (Vermilion). 91: Kate Grenville, *The Idea of Perfection* (Picador). 93: Nick Hornby, *How to be Good* (Penguin). 94: Elizabeth Von Arnim, *The Enchanted April* (Virago). 96: Libby Purves, *Holy Smoke* (Hodder & Stoughton). 97: David Stephen, *String Lug the Fox* (Lutterworth). 98: David Nobbs, *Second from the Last in the Sack Race* (Mandarin). 100: Sarah Litvinoff, *The Relate Guide to Better Relationships* (Vermilion). 101: Esther de Waal, *Seeking God* (HarperCollins). 102: Kate Grenville, *The Idea of Perfection* (Picador). 103: Steve Turner, *Nice and Nasty* (Marshall, Morgan & Scott). 104: Willa Cather, *My Antonia* (Virago). 105: Johann Wolfgang von Goethe, 'Song from the Watch Tower', translated by David Luke. 108: Gladys Hunt, *Honey for a Child's Heart* (Zondervan). 108: Paul Brand & Philip Yancey, *Fearfully and Wonderfully Made* (Hodder & Stoughton). 109: Used by permission of the author. 110: Ann Lewin, *Candles and Kingfishers* (Methodist Publishing House). Used by permission of the author. 111: Johann Christoph Arnold, *The Lost Art of Forgiveness* (The Plough Publishing House). 112: Ian McEwan, *Black Dogs* (Vintage). 113: Luci Shaw, *Postcard from the Shore* (Highland Books, 1985). 114: Elizabeth Von Arnim, *The Enchanted April* (Virago). 115: Used by permission of Cherry Greveson. 116: Philip Hallie, *Lest Innocent Blood Be Shed* (Harper Perennial). 117: John Grisham, *The Testament* (Arrow). 118: Susan Hill, *A Change for the Better* (Penguin). 119: Jacqueline Wilson, *Girls Under Pressure* (Corgi Books). 120: Victor Hugo, *Les Misérables* (Penguin). 122: Anne Tyler, *Saint Maybe* (Vintage). 122: Frederick Buechner, *Now and Then* (Harper & Row, 1983). 126: Used by permission of the author. 126: Tove Jansson, *The Exploits of Moominpappa* (Morrow,William & Company). 127: Used by permission of the author. 42, 43, 64, 65, 121: Scripture quotations taken from the *Holy Bible, New International Version*, copyright (c) 1973, 1978, 1984 by International Bible Society. Used by permission of Hodder & Stoughton Limited. All rights reserved. 'NIV' is a registered trademark of International Bible Society. UK trademark number 1448790.